Ask
Mother Nature
A Conscious Gardener's Guide

Ask
Mother Nature
A Conscious Gardener's Guide

Ellen Vande Visse

FINDHORN PRESS

Published in 2009 by Findhorn Press, Scotland

ISBN 978-1-84409-163-8

Edited by Michael Hawkins
Cover, interior design and illustrations by Damian Keenan
Printed and bound in the USA

1 2 3 4 5 6 7 8 9 10 11 12 14 13 12 11 10 09

Published by
Findhorn Press
305a The Park, Findhorn
Forres IV36 3TE
Scotland, UK

Telephone
+44-(0)1309-690582
Fax
+44-(0)131-777-2177

info@findhornpress.com
www.findhornpress.com

Contents

Contents

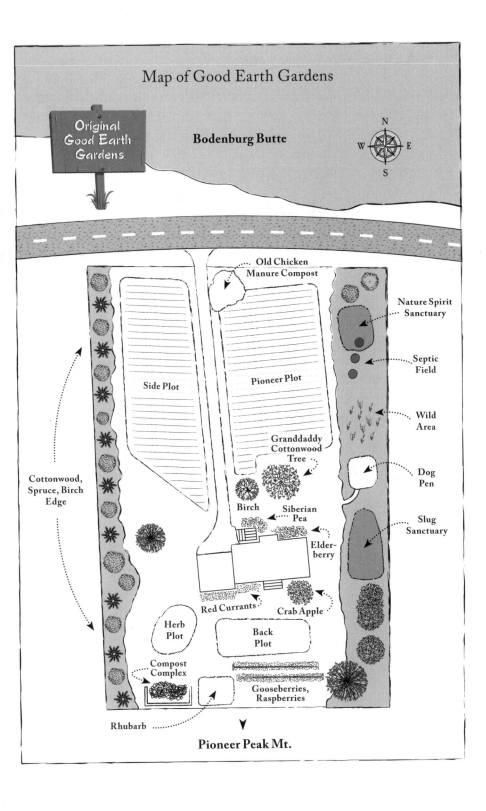

Map of Good Earth Gardens

Original Good Earth Gardens

Bodenburg Butte

N
W E
S

Old Chicken Manure Compost

Nature Spirit Sanctuary

Septic Field

Side Plot

Pioneer Plot

Wild Area

Granddaddy Cottonwood Tree

Dog Pen

Cottonwood, Spruce, Birch Edge

Birch

Siberian Pea

Elder-berry

Slug Sanctuary

Red Currants

Crab Apple

Herb Plot

Back Plot

Compost Complex

Gooseberries, Raspberries

Rhubarb

Pioneer Peak Mt.

Opening Prayer

It is my hope and my prayer that:

What follows will inspire you to converse, cooperate, and co-create with the great beings of nature.

My stories help direct you towards a kinder, more harmonious way of living cooperatively with all the other species on the planet.

My experiences will help you with the practical matters of applying conscious cooperation in your daily life. This narrative inspires you to tune in and receive spiritual guidance.

This book helps you to connect deeper with your soul and re-bond with the soul of Mother Earth.

These episodes add to the growing pool of knowledge that helps us humans fully reclaim our inner divinity and our sacred working relationship with the Devic and Elemental kingdoms.

Maggot Attack!

I STEP into the broccoli patch and scratch my head. How can this be? I could swear that the broccoli were taller last week. Am I hallucinating? Why would plants shrink? I check the cauliflower sections of the garden: it's the same disappearing act.

Each morning I return to inspect. These seedlings ARE definitely shrinking instead of growing. In fact, whole beds of broccoli and cauliflower plants have shriveled from 6 down to 3 (15.24 to 7.62cm) They are limp and turning a sickly purple color. My two big cash crops are rapidly expiring.

I pull up a few plants. What? No roots? Where are they? I finally yank out a plant with a few remaining roots. The roots are crawling with animated white rice grains.

I ask experienced gardeners, and learn that the culprits are root maggots. Which kind? Whether the species are technically turnip maggot (root fly), cabbage maggot or corn seed maggot, they look alike and specialize in devouring entire root systems of the cabbage or mustard family. Ironically, the crops that grow well in Alaska's cool climate are the crops that are vulnerable: cauliflower, broccoli, cabbage, Brussels sprouts, kohlrabi, and radish.

Experts explain that these maggots are the larval stage of their life cycle. How did they get here? The adult form is a fly, and can sense where to go for successful procreation. When I wasn't looking a couple weeks ago, those sneaky flies zeroed in on my broccoli and cauliflower babies and laid their tiny eggs. Their eggs quickly hatched and squirmed down to the root systems, where I find them now, cleverly executing their mission underground. I've discovered ravenous gangs of white larvae. Are they in all my other cole (brassica) or crucifer crops as well?

These root maggots are sucking down my rows of tender transplants like underground vacuum cleaners. They are sucking my profits under as well. I'm depending on these cole crops to carry me through the cold Alaskan winter, both for our home food supply and for income from selling surplus. The maggots are literally eating me out of house and home.

I'm desperate. "Do as I do," my neighbor suggests. "Sprinkle the pesticide Diazinon in the soil before you plant. That's what works." The Cooperative Extension Service bulletin says I can rescue-spray right now with the insecticide Lorsban or Dursban (chlorpyrifos), but my customers expect only organic vegetables. And at this rate I won't have any vegetables. How do I stop this voracious population of root-gobbling maggots?

I don't have a clue. Everything here is new to me — root maggots, Alaska growing conditions, and commercial market gardening.

Nothing in my past life in Michigan has prepared me for this. My training was in biology/ecology. I served as an environmental education consultant, training students and school teachers to become more ecologically conscious and re-bond with nature. After eleven years I got the yen for Alaska — more wildness and more cross-country skiing. I moved to Anchorage, restlessly doing odd jobs for my first two years. Then a friend gave me a copy of *The Findhorn Garden*. Hair stood up on the back of my neck.

I had to see this place in Scotland where people consulted with spirits of nature for garden advice, where pilgrims came to marvel at giant vegetables in wind-swept sand dune, and roses bloomed in the snow.

Co-founder Dorothy Maclean, I read, communicated with the soul of soil, herbs, and insects. She tapped into an angel-like consciousness behind each expression of nature. She called these great spiritual beings Devas, and they gave her practical guidance. They told her when to transplant and how to fertilize. When pests took over, Dorothy and others in this Findhorn group somehow asked them to ease up on their vegetable damage. It was all about cooperation and communication.

I dropped everything and flew to Scotland to witness this Findhorn Community first hand. Dorothy was no longer living there, and the vegetables had calmed down to normal size after making their point that human attitudes affect growth. Yet I was taken by the peacefulness of the place, and the gardens bursting with productivity. A surge of passion swept away the controlled order of my scientific mind. I burst out with a spontaneous shout, "I crave soil. I want to farm. I want to grow gardens the way they do at Findhorn!"

Back in Alaska, I immediately teamed with two other Alaskan immigrants,

Fay Wilder and Jim Strohmer, who were educational colleagues from my Environmental Education work in Michigan. Together, we bought a house on almost two acres near Palmer in the fertile Matanuska Valley. We plowed up the sprawling lawn and I started planting.

So here I am in my own Good Earth Gardens, only a few weeks into farming, and I am confronting my first crisis. I have no idea what to do about broccoli-infesting root maggots. Findhorn inspired me, but gave me no hands-on training on how to actually communicate with nature beings.

I ponder how to go about this. How do I partner with nature? Do I pray? Do I use organic controls? Or do I apply advice from the newest book I've been given? In *Behaving as If the God in All Things Mattered*, Author Machaelle Small Wright writes how she tells a certain pest that it may only take the first plant in each row. This is appealing. No need for killing and warfare. Simply set limits on what the pests can consume.

I stride into the garden to try this.

First Communications

I WALK in a circle around the broccoli and cauliflower beds. Aloud, I ask for the turnip root maggots' attention. While I am at it, I include cutworms (caterpillars) — just in case they become a problem to me too. I announce to the Devas of these two insects that they can only take the first plant in each row. Thank you very much!

Every day, I hurry out to check progress. What is this? I find MORE victims of the root maggots. Furthermore, the dead and dying cole plants are conspicuously NOT the first ones in each row. I continue my daily body count, and I keep finding still more withered, sickly broccoli and cauliflower. By early June, rows and rows are looking desolate. Very few healthy plants still survive. Aagh! This is an unacceptable level of damage.

Didn't the root maggot Deva hear me? Don't the insect larvae want to co-operate with me? I threaten to quit growing broccoli and cauliflower crops ever again. I thought I had applied Ms. Wright's technique correctly. This should have worked.

I am perplexed. Why isn't my proclamation getting results? What language do these larvae speak? I feel like I am addressing peculiar characters in a foreign country. Yet the book *Behaving as If the God in All Things Mattered* emphatically claimed that everyone can do this conversing and get results.

Our short growing season has advanced to June 10, and root maggots still ravage on. I realize that I need to enlist some assistance. My passion surpasses my fear of sounding completely daft, and I boldly recruit my housemate Jim Strohmer plus Shawn Knudeson who is here visiting. Apparently our friendship allows them to go along with this. They do not seem to think it odd to have a chat with a root-devouring maggot. I probably have more doubts about myself than Jim and Shawn do.

First, I explain my dilemma. I pour out my story and share my disappointment over my lack of results. "Was that a request or an order you gave the root maggots?" asks Jim. I stammer. Jim presses further, "Did you open a two-way conversation with them?"

"Not exactly," I confess. "I told them what I wanted. I just expected that they would agree with me.

"Didn't Machaelle Small Wright's book emphasize treating the insects as equal members of a fellow civilization?" wonders Shawn.

"Okay, I say skeptically. I guess I did come on as a superior human concerned only with making a profit."

"And they ignored you."

"Totally."

We laugh.

The three of us sit down on the living room floor. My chest tightens and my underarms moisten. Quiet suspense hangs in the air as Jim and Shawn look at me. With doubt and trepidation, I suggest that we start with an invocation. "Deva of the root maggots eating my cole crops," I venture, "may we three humans be in conscious connection with you?" I pause awkwardly, not sure if this Deva wants to join us.

"First," I continue, "would you please give us a sense of what you are like as the Deva?"

My silent companions must have a clear hook-up. Both of them start reporting impressions coming into their minds. Shawn senses the personality of the root maggots. She feels them laugh with a ho, ho, ho. She perceives that these beings are stalwart and hold a deep-rooted love for the Earth. She simultaneously becomes aware that this maggot consciousness is annoyed. This Deva does not like being labeled and persecuted as a "pest." Shawn says that the Deva appreciates my love for the Earth. Therefore this root maggot consciousness is willing to consider my request to take only the first plant in each row.

Jim adds the perspective he received: *"Keep in mind that we are always in the soil. There's no option of simply eliminating us. We are always present in the soil."*

Whew! I flood with immense gratitude and relief. The maggots had heard me, after all. I ask the Deva, "Is there anything I can do for you?"

"Yes," I hear with a chuckle, *"take out the marigolds!"* I had replaced deceased broccoli plants with marigolds, and this Deva humorously acknowledges that

marigold roots are distasteful. *"Seriously,"* adds the Deva, *"You can most help yourselves, me, and the garden by learning to love me as much as you love the other Devas and the land."*

I generate a third question. It occurs to me that I had told two kinds of pests (root maggots AND cutworms) that they could eat the first vegetable at the beginning of each row. "Would you like me to tell the cutworms that they can eat the last plant in each row? That would reserve the first plant in the rows for you exclusively. Would this arrangement be more comfortable for you?"

Shawn felt/heard a voice in her head say, *"Thanks for your concern. You're not bad for humans!"*

Jim's final impression from the Deva is, *"Don't be discouraged. Be persistent. Keep loving the land."*

These maggot beings are confident, jocular, and very proud of the role they play in the ecosystem. They are very amused by my halting attempts to communicate.

We follow Machaelle Small Wright's formula for closing the conversation by figuratively "hanging up the phone". We address the Deva of Turnip Root Maggots by saying, "Thank you! We disconnect with you now."

Wow! We have successfully accomplished a direct conversation. And these beings are nice to me. In fact, they are full of fun. I am encouraged.

Now, will they spare my remaining crops?

Closer Encounters:
Call Me Charlie...

IT IS NOW late June, and nothing has changed. In fact, infestation is worse than ever. I even find root maggots damaging the green beans. I develop three problems. First, I'm very angry. I cannot imagine conjuring up enough friendliness to engage in a conversation and ask them to back off... again. They are killing my adolescent plants that I've mothered along since I sowed their seeds indoors in March. It's personal!

Second, I am repulsed. I become fixated on the image of the wounded ones, dying in the sun, all sickly and discolored. When I pull up the afflicted broccoli, cauliflower, and bean stalks, the stumps writhe with squirming larvae. My stomach goes queasy. It's difficult to feel loving toward something so repulsive. Third, I question their sense of fair play and willingness to cooperate. It appears that the root maggots do not want to cooperate. I'm feeling totally offended.

All my pent-up frustrations spill out on Jan Pohl when she stops by after work on June 30th. Fay, Jan, and I have been having such fun teaching together in the Trailside Discovery Camp program here in the Matanuska Valley. I spout my anguish about my cole plants and failed attempts at spiritual gardening. Fortunately Jan receives my emotive stories using her Quaker neutrality. And then, with her usual wise and playful character, she smiles and exclaims, "Oh, I'm intrigued with your project, Ellie. Let's talk to those root maggots! I'm excited!"

Boosted by Jan's bravery, Fay is also willing to try. The three of us quiet our minds and begin our attempt.

I speak for our group. "Deva of Turnip Root Maggots, we are new at this, but we ask to be in conscious connection with you. We are learning to recognize your larval form in the garden, eating the roots of mustard family members. Is that your species I see damaging the green beans, as well? There are so many of you that your numbers are seriously damaging my crops intended for market. We want to talk with you about this."

Turnip Maggot Deva, eagerly and enthusiastically: *Ah, it is good, good, good, that you are getting to know us. Yes, that's us in the beans, too.*

Fay: Why?

Turnip Maggot Deva: Because we are very hungry. We suggest you plant more beets everywhere.

Ellen: Why are you present in such enormous numbers? You are maintaining a very high population level.

Turnip Maggot Deva: *That's because you need us.*

Jan: Why?

Turnip Maggot Deva: *We are your teacher. You've been asking to learn more about communication with Devas. We are just the teacher you need to start learning.*

Jan: Why?

Turnip Maggot Deva: *We are easy for you to communicate with. We are willing to spend time with you. We'll help you learn how to communicate. We have more of an out-going personality than some of the other devas. Just don't expect to harvest too many beans this round. But do not get discouraged or worry. By the way, you can call us "Charlie."* (This was said with a feeling of great exuberance.)

We immediately think of a boy, Charlie Burke, one of our students at the Trailside science camp. We laugh with delight, just thinking of him. When Charlie smiles, his whole face lights up. If Charlie aims his sunshine smile at you, you find it impossible to think of one problem in the whole world for that moment. His spontaneous joy holds you in a time-stopping trance.

Ellen: Hmm, "Charlie?" Address you, the Deva of Turnip Maggots, as "Charlie"? I do have quite a problem trying to love your form. I'm instantly sickened when I think of root balls of writhing maggots and withering broccoli. Yes, it would make it easier to call you Charlie. This way, I will try to see you as the happy kid Charlie, whirling around the plants, dancing, and having a good time!

Fay: Why do you recommend that we plant more beets?

Charlie (the Turnip Root Maggot Deva): *Because people like beets. The beets will show something. Put them everywhere.*

To tell the truth, when you first asked about beans, I was just so happy I just wanted to say something, because I was so excited to have contact with you. So I said, "plant beets". We root maggots are happy, happy, happy that you humans are talking with us. More beets, more beets, more beets!

Ellen: What wonderful enthusiasm! Now I am getting a feeling of being fed too much at once. I see a picture of a string. What is the string about?

Charlie: *I didn't send it.*

Fay: Who did?

Charlie: *I don't know.*

Fay: Is it from a good source, that is, from truth, light, and love?

Answer from unidentified source: *Yes. There are other good minds at work here too, and we are eager to help you.*

Ellen: Oh. Well then, hello to you! Welcome! What does the string mean?

Answer: *It means that you can only understand and absorb so much at one sitting. So, it's like picking up the end of a string and following a long trail, in small installments. You will see and understand as you go along. You will learn the communication, a little at a time. We are happy and playful, and so glad to be acknowledged and consulted. Enjoy working your way along the string.*

Ellen: Great! Thanks. We still wonder about the beets. Why plant more and where? As we feel for an answer, Fay remarks that she feels and senses beets, and feels remarkably energized.

Jan: What does that mean?

Charlie and the other devas present: *Ha, ha, ha, hee, hee! That was a little joke. Fay was "beat" and needed a boost. So we gave her beet energy. She'll need a nap after this session. She's been working hard. We love her!*

Ellen: What is important for us to realize or understand next?

Charlie: *Now when you dig up a cluster of root maggots, think of them as a whole bundle of little Charlies! It is very important to see us as little Charlies when you see us in the garden, rather than "pests".*

Jan and Fay received the essence of this communication in words. Mine is wordless. I feel emotional, like someone is clawing dirt out from the center of my heart.

We feel like the conversation is concluding. Then Jan gets a parting shot from Deva Charlie. *"We're going to back off on our consumption of the bean crop somewhat. We hadn't planned to, but we are feeling affectionate towards you."*

We close with a great big thank you to Charlie and to the other devas who joined us. I repeat my vow to practice thinking of Charlie Burke's smile whenever I see those little white maggots in the soil. We disconnect, still glowing from the good will and cheers we were given. I am amazed — when Fay, Jan, and I combined our efforts, we received extensive elaboration by pooling our impressions.

Personally, I am ecstatic. A representative of the animal kingdom has graciously volunteered to coach me — the human, the fledgling gardener, the novice communicator. What's next? Will I see evidence of the turnip root maggot population in retreat?

❦

As July progresses, several more cole and bean individuals succumb, but Charlie's lesson in attitudes keeps me from submerging into despair. At the same time, Alaska's long hours of daylight stimulate the beans, broccoli, and cauliflower to grow faster than maggots can destroy them. Damaged plants begin to recover and flourish.

The August and September gardening phases command my attention, and my pace accelerates into a headlong sprint to care for and harvest the other 25 kinds of crops. These varieties yield well and supplement the overall sales nicely. I am too busy to dwell on losses. I forget about root maggots and Charlie, and his offer to be my Devic Ambassador. I rest for the winter and walk blindly into the next planting season.

Trap Crops

ANOTHER PLANTING season arrives at Good Earth Gardens, and I contract a serious disease. It happens each and every spring. This malaise is called amnesia, or "Gardener's Blind Enthusiasm Syndrome".

I am filled with optimism. I dream of Bigger and Better. I'm intoxicated by the energizing sunlight and warmth. I forget last year's exhaustion and hard work. In particular, I blithely set out bed after bed of cute broccoli, cauliflower, and cabbage transplants, mindless of previous problems.

After all, I have developed new markets. My customers are especially eager for cole crops. These vegetables are hefty and folks pay by the pound. I know these will sell well. It seems like I can grow an endless supply.

I have two years of experience behind me now. I'm eager to see positive cash flow. I dare to anticipate actually making a partial living this summer from my market garden.

Augh! What is this?!? This morning's inspection shocks me. Several cole plants are withered and purple. I find several more dying over here. And several more over there. This is the trademark of the root maggot. Are these pests in full force, again? Does this mean disaster for my business and another huge crop loss this season? Ye gods, what do I do now?

I strain to peer back through my hazy memory... what had the Turnip Maggot Deva told me? I recall something about Charlie and "plant more beets!" Right now I most remember my discouragement; strongly. Last year, I had high losses of crucifer family crops early in the season. Has Charlie forgotten our agreement for this year?

What would that Charlie recommend now, with infestation rapidly rising? Can I even make contact and ask the Deva, especially on my own?

Last year's talk with Charlie was with a group of supportive friends. When I try to communicate solo, I am skeptical and distrustful of the thoughts I receive. I feel extreme shakiness and low confidence. In short, I suffer from a common malady that keeps most people from consulting with pests: I simply doubt that I can do it.

It's late and I'm pooped! I'll think about this tomorrow. Maybe a miracle solution will pop up.

Ah, a new day. Hey, what's this? Unexpected help rolls into the driveway. Miracles do happen! My dear friends Janice and Ed Schofield are surprising me with a visit from Homer. Jan is a wild herb author, teacher, and fellow spiritual seeker.

"Hi, Ed! Hey, Janice!" I blurt, hardly giving them time to get out of the auto. "How about coming out to the garden with me? I need your expert consultation. The vegetables are off to a good start, but the pests are off to even a better one. Would you walk down the rows with me, and help me do a check up? Jan, would you bring your pendulum?" I know Janice uses a pendulum as a tool when she's confronted with a multitude of questions. She poses one question at a time, and the pendulum enhances her intuition to indicate an answer. Today I'm riddled with questions.

I show Janice the shrunken sickly broccoli plants. "A few days ago they were bright green," I tell her. "Now look — many of my young plants are in the throes of death. The turnip root maggots have eaten all their roots."

"Let's find out what's going on," says Jan. "Let's check in with their head honcho."

"Deva of the Turnip Root Maggot," I begin, "we seek your cooperation and communication."

"We would like to work with you," Jan chimes in, "so that Ellie may have a productive garden, and you may have what your species needs."

Jan feels her attention drawn to the empty spaces in the broccoli rows. Here, individual plants had succumbed and I had removed them. "I feel a lack of larvae in this space," says Janice. "Do you recommend that Ellie plant something else there?"

The pendulum swings side to side. "This means *yes* in my communication scheme," explains Janice. "Each person has to establish the *yes* and *no* signal with his/her tool."

"What would you like to ask, Ellie? We need to ask YES/NO questions with the pendulum."

"What am I to plant in these spaces?"

Jan jots a list and tests with her pendulum. She asks aloud if Ellie is to plant:

- Replacement broccoli?   No
- Companion plants?   Yes
- Garlic?   No
- Onions   Yes
- Marigolds?   Yes

"I am getting a sense that the Turnip Maggot Deva is not willing to leave completely at this time," says Jan. "Wait a minute." Jan stops. She scribbles madly on her pad, pauses, and says, "This is how I would interpret what I got." *The reason is partly because of Ellie's beliefs. She believes that we root maggots can leave merely at her request, but she doesn't believe totally that we will. So we won't.*

"I also asked them," continues Janice, "if they had other reasons for being in this garden in rather high proportions? This is what they told me, as I piece together impressions."

We like it here. There's no toxic junk. Some of us will leave though, in the spirit of cooperation. We will increase our cooperation (in leaving) each year.

I'm receiving another message," Jan tells me. The Deva is saying, *"We want a crop for ourselves".*

She tests again with the pendulum.

- Turnip? It swings left and right, which is her message for *no*.
- Radish? She gets an enthusiastic forward and back swing. "That means *yes*," Jan relays to me.

"Will the turnip root maggot leave some radishes for Ellie?" Jan queries. Her answer comes partly from watching the pendulum and part from a gut feeling. *Yes, we will share. We will spare some*, respond the root maggots.

"What should be done with the infested radishes?" Jan continues.

- leave them in place?   No
- take them to the dump?   No
- compost them?   Yes

"Well, Jan," I splutter, "this is new to me, but I will start it tomorrow. Right now, my mind is jumping to several other crops and problems. Would you help me check the rest of the garden? I'm wondering about some other puzzling signs."

A Dowser in
the Garden

"WHAT OTHER mysteries do you have," Jan asks? "Well, cutworms," I quickly respond. "I'm worried about cutworms. I've had trouble with them in the past — are they about to appear in droves and fell my tender transplants again?"

"What are cutworms?" asks Jan.

"They are chubby, juicy caterpillars. About as long as a joint in your finger. Most cutworms are brown and difficult to spot on the soil. Cutworms can mow down rows and rows of young vegetables in just a few nights," I spout. My animation accelerates.

"Cutworms are fattening up now, just when my rows of seed crops are germinating and my hundreds of transplants are trying to get a foothold. Cutworms operate at night, crawling along the soil until they come to a stem of a plant. They wrap themselves around the stem, right at the base. They eat out the flesh. They march on to the next tender stem and the next. Plants topple over. In the morning all I find are the wilted fatalities in the morning.

"I imagine the night air resounding with cutworms yelling "Timmmmber!" like a team of lumberjacks. I see them settle down to delectable vegetarian banquets. They gorge their bellies. Then, with a contented burp, they burrow under the soil to sleep it off in the morning."

"I can see you have a bit of energy around cutworms. Do you want to work out a cooperative agreement with them, Ellie?" asks Janice. Her calm objectivity brings me back from all my pent-up fears.

"Oh, right. Yes, I do."

Janice, being the neutral party, leads the invocation. "Hello, great spirit of cutworms. We would like to check in with you. Ellie wants to work with you instead of attack you like pests. What should Ellie be doing to cooperate with you and your population?"

Jan reports the simple reply of, *We are not a significant problem at this time.* We both have a hearty laugh. I had built up all that anxiety for nothing!

"What else would you like to check in with, Ellie?" asks Jan.

I scan my "worry spots" in the garden. "Right now I would like to consult with celery, green beans, cauliflower, head lettuce, and one birch tree."

Janice walks from crop to crop, assessing with her intuition-plus-pendulum style of attunement..

"Celery, what do you need to optimize growth that Ellie can provide?"

We are happy. We don't need anything.

"Green beans, do you need anything?"

(with hyped-up excitement) *We lack nutrients. We want sunshine. Feed us compost as a side dressing or in liquid form as compost tea.*

"Cauliflower, how are you doing, in the light of root maggot problems in your cousins, the broccoli."

We appreciate the marigolds you've planted with us.

We don't have any special needs right now.

Notice our vibrant green color.

(The Deva conveys this message with lilting voice and dancing spirit.)

"Head lettuce, how about you?"

(In a tone that sounds like an eager child)

We want some fish emulsion!

"Birch tree by the house, we understand that your leaves become brown-tipped each summer. The Cooperative Extension Service expert said it was due to pesticides applied elsewhere, and carried onto you by the breezes. The term is "drift". Is this true?"

Yes, it is caused by a pesticide, and not by anything done by Ellie or the household.

"What do you need?" we ask. "What would you like?"

We are still strong. One or several things would benefit us, but are not essential to rescue or "save" us.

- Fish emulsion?	*Yes*
- Compost?	*Yes*
- Flowers around your base?	*Yes*
- Clip dead branch ends?	*If you want to*
- Lots of water	*Yes*

I soar with buoyant enthusiasm. We thank the Devas and close. I thank Janice, explaining, "I appreciate working with you. Your second opinion and your additional insights sure help boost my confidence."

And to myself I mutter, "I wonder how I will ever be able to talk to these beings in the garden by myself when Jan and Ed go back to Homer?"

Becoming an Avid Trapper

THE DAY AFTER the Schofields depart, I side-dress the green beans and give the head lettuce a meal of fish emulsion.

Then, with great resolve, I grab a bag of bulk radish seed and plant a circle of seed around each broccoli and cauliflower bed. As I sow, I ask the fly stage of the root maggot to choose these radishes that I am providing for their egg-laying, rather than broccoli and cauliflower plants.

I keenly monitor growth over the next few weeks. As soon as the radish seeds sprout and their tops reach 6-10" (15.24 to 25.4cm) high, I yank out all these radish plants bordering each bed. At this stage the roots are becoming slightly bulbous. On most of the radishes' red and white flesh, I find gray spots, distorted shapes, and an unappetizing look. This is the work of the maggots. Thus I am a successful new trapper, capturing the root maggots. Ta Da.

The radishes, instead of the broccoli and cauliflower, have attracted the turnip flies. I dump the infested radishes into the compost pile. The root maggots will die there as their radish hosts expire. Since they starve in larval stage, they will never become adult flies able to lay eggs.

I immediately re-sow the vacated rows with fresh radish seed and repeat the strategy. I happily sacrifice the radishes in order to lure and trap the pests.

The broccoli and cauliflower inside the ring of radishes grow bigger and bigger without signs of damage. I reap ample harvest as the season climaxes. The dowsing indeed proves accurate. The crucial requirement is timing. My job must be to sow radishes before or immediately after setting out cole crops, since the adult flies can zero-in on any of the crucifers as soon as they are brought outdoors.

I learn later that this is an established tactic, and it has a name: it is called planting a trap crop. Perhaps trap-cropping is a familiar practice to experienced organic gardeners, but I am not one.

I monitor the cutworm activity as well. As the season unfolds, I see that the cutworms told the truth: their population never becomes a significant problem. Only one year in twelve did I see the cutworm population explode into infestation levels, and even then, cutworms were not numerous in my garden. When I raked my fingers through a square foot (100cm^2) of soil in my neighbor's field, I counted 30 cutworms in one stroke. *"We're starving!"* they told me. That was the only season I used collars, hand-picking, and other management tools available to organic growers.

Watching the celery, beans, cauliflower, and lettuce makes me smile, because they are maturing nicely. As for the birch tree, we start watering it regularly, and transplant four marigolds under its canopy. At first, I react with a feeling of futility, saying, "This is silly, there is nothing we can do to negate the toxic chemical residue."

Then I review *The Findhorn Garden* book. It reminds me that this is actually a very positive action. We humans are showing love by encouraging the birch to be strong. We are giving it the positive attention of some bright, happy marigold companions.

I continue to observe that birch tree. Over several years it has grown steadily, and each summer its leaves show less browning than the year before. With all this verification, I am beginning to trust this Devic guidance stuff.

How to Collar a Cutworm

When cutworm populations are significantly high, several management strategies are available. Organic options include: hand-picking, barriers like collars and floating row covers, cultivation, timing, inter-cropping, leaving the weeds, crop rotation, diatomaceous earth, and a biological control like Bt or a beneficial nematode. *Please see Appendix 1-B.*

Broccoli:
We Fight Cancer

I SNAG MY unsuspecting friend who stops by on a cloudy day in mid-July. "Come to the garden with me," I beckon. "I'd like to check in with the broccoli and see how it's doing."

"Huh?" queries Cheryl. "Do you mean you want me to help you inspect something?"

"I had some problems earlier in my broccoli beds." I explain. "I have pest and fertilizer challenges. I can see the above-surface leaves and stems, but I want to know about their overall well-being, and I become like an over-anxious parent...."

"And what do you want me to do?" she asks.

"I want you to help me talk to them — to ask if they are having any problems." I see Cheryl's puzzled expression. "You want ME to help you talk to some plants?"

"Yes, it's easy." I exude cheer and confidence, hoping to convince myself as well. "I'll show you as we go along."

Cheryl shrugs and nods. "Okay, I'll help if I can."

"I call this process tuning in, or a tune-in," I explain. "According to experts at the Findhorn Garden in Scotland, every plant, every rock, and every place has a collective consciousness. Some call it an angel or Deva, meaning a Being of Light. So we begin by saying hello and asking this overlighting spirit to communicate with us.

"Broccoli Deva," I venture, "Cheryl and I would like to thank you for being present and holding the energy of these broccoli varieties here. We would like to attune and communicate with you."

"As we proceed," I say to Cheryl, "imagine in your mind the feel, smell, and appearance of broccoli. Recall the taste of its green florets, raw and cooked. We let our analytical thoughts go silent. This is the time to make note of anything that comes to your mind — pictures, emotions, music, images, impressions, words. Everyone gets information differently and one way is not superior to another. Just trust and report what you receive."

"Trust whatever you get, Ellie, " I remind myself inwardly. "Let your skepticism go."

"I get a sense of a very sweet personality," says Cheryl.

"I'm feeling a subtle energy shift, too. I think we are connected. Let's ask how the broccoli is doing."

"I got a sense of *Yes, we are doing fine,*" says Cheryl.

"Me too," I add. ("Whew," I think to myself, "this is working! Together we are getting an answer.")

The next part is strange. I expect to hear about root maggots and soil nutrition. Instead, Cheryl gets words: *Does my personality seem sweet and casual? Ah, don't be fooled. We broccoli are very strong. We fight cancer when you partake of us. We are very proud of this!*

We look at each other in astonishment. (This was not a well-known fact in 1989.) I never know what I am going to learn from a conversation with a green plant. What I do know is that it pays to boldly recruit innocent bystanders. Zeal and assistance help me overcome my feelings of incompetence.

Fertilizers – Broccoli Advises a No-No

YIPPEE, RECOVERY! The root maggot damage is subsiding! The remaining broccoli are filling out, heading up, producing nice yields. I love this kind of gardening. Ask the Devas and get results. It's a joy... till now.

On this mid-August day, I expectantly grab my knife to start slicing picture-perfect broccoli... but wait! I can only find heads the size of quarters. Where are those meaty, sprawling, show-off broccoli now? I was planning on having great harvests for another six weeks.

I want MORE. I want BIGGER. And I want it CONTINUOUSLY until freeze-up! How? I'm still such a kindergartner that I don't even know how to look up this kind of horticultural information.

I guess I'd best ask the broccoli itself, but inquiring all by myself still scares me. My un-aided communiqués' with Devas produce vague snippets of information and heaps of doubts. Janice had suggested I try a pendulum. Others like Machaelle Small Wright use kinesiology (muscle testing) with great success. I'm frustrated because those methods only produce answers for simple yes/no questions. I want details. I want elaboration. I want to learn more background.

I'm no psychic. Maybe I need to recruit a friend again. Fay, my housemate, is an obvious target. Here is a happy, calm soul who has minimal ego need and personal agenda. This means she is a terrific listener with no need to impose her own opinions over the guidance coming through from angelic sources.

"Fay, I'd love to have you help me have a conversation with the Deva of Broccoli".

"Sure," she says brightly. We sit on the edge of the broccoli bed, armed with pencils and paper. "Tell me exactly what you want to ask so I can focus on your questions."

I scratch my head, then put some key words on paper.

Fay, meanwhile, sits with eyes closed, inhaling deeply. "It smells so green, so alive. And I am remembering delicious broccoli on white dinner plates, steaming with aroma."

"Hello and highest greetings!" I call aloud to the Broccoli Deva. "We thank you for growing here. We seek your guidance. Would you advise us about how to help you grow bigger broccoli heads, please? What nutrients can we add to perk up production and vigor here? We want to finish the season with buckets and buckets of those heavy-weight broccoli."

We wait in silence. My mind bounces with doubts. I know so little about fertilizers. I strain my brain, dig for answers, and tense as I try.

I peek at Fay — she looks relaxed and accepting of whatever floats into her mind. After a few moments, we compare impressions.

"Fay, I am getting only one word: 'nitrogen', I confess. I doubt its accuracy.

"Me, too," she says.

"Really? I'm not just making this up?" I feel my body settle down.

"Apparently not. Maybe you could ask for details."

"Broccoli Deva," I continue, "do you have a preference for the nitrogen source? I have blood meal and fish emulsion on hand."

"And *Miracle Gro*," chimes Fay. "You have all that nitrogen power in the back of the shed." (*Miracle Gro* is a common garden and houseplant fertilizer. It's a water-soluble blue powder.)

"Oh, come on Fay, that's not organic."

"No, but there is bit left from the first year when you were a chemical gardener. You do have it available."

"Okay, we can add humor to this tune-in. Blood meal, yes or no?"

I watch as Fay scribbles. Then she reports, "I heard the Broccoli Deva say, *Yes, that's fine. Make it into a tea and water it in around the base of the broccoli. Include a blessing to each plant as you apply.*"

"And fish emulsion?"

Fay listens, then relays what she received. *Yes, this is fine too. Again, give a blessing as you put it on.*

"And *Miracle Gro*?" I ask, laughing.

Fay listens again, and shakes her head in disbelief. "What I heard is, *Well, let's have a miracle. Yes!*" It came into my head with great fun and enthusiasm.

"Seriously, won't its chemicals harm the soil?" I question.

"The Deva is telling me," continues Fay, "*that Miracle Gro would work quickly in our cold Alaskan soils and give the boost so critically needed at this time. Since we are feeding the soil all that compost and doing regular organic soil management, there is no soil harm from this one short-term use."*

"Are you sure, Fay?"

"That's what came through."

"Well, okay if you say so. I don't know how I'd tell anyone that my organic crop got a chemical boost."

"Broccoli Deva, what do you advise about nitrogen for next year's broccoli crops?" I ask. "I want to prevent this deficiency next year. What amount of nitrogen do you recommend as I initially prepare the garden soil?"

Fay quiets again, then reports, *Whatever you usually use for your nitrogen sources, double it for your broccoli beds. The same is true for cabbage, kale, and cauliflower. Add an ample potassium source as well.*

"I am glad to learn this, Broccoli Deva. I'll go ahead and use *Miracle Gro* immediately, and make a note about next season's fertilizers. Thank you so much. I think that's all the questions I have for now. Thank you so much for talking with us. We close our connection with gratitude."

I leap to my feet. I grab Fay's hands and haul her up, doing a little jig. "We've done it, we've done it!" I shout. "Our tune-ins are working. The Devas are talking to us, taking us step by step!"

I skip to the shed and haul out the jar of blue *Miracle Gro* crystals, plus hose, measuring spoon, and pump sprayer. "Egad, I hope no one sees the secret miracle. Fay, if anyone asks, tell them that a Deva made me do it."

I merrily drench the soil and leaves in each broccoli bed. "Don't forget the blessing," Fay reminds me.

"May you do miracles!" I sing out as I spray.

Two weeks later, I discover some fist-sized heads in the broccoli beds. Each week, I gratefully and progressively harvest more and more. As the season draws to a close, I realize that I have harvested four times the poundage (2kg) of broccoli as I expected.

"It's a miracle," I tell Fay. "That Deva provided accurate counsel. I admit that I have been asking myself, "Why, when we ask for guidance, do we then doubt and discount it?"'"

"Yes, and a miracle that you believed the guidance and did what the Deva recommended. This was a good test, because *Miracle Gro* was not something your mind would have said. It had to be from the Devas themselves. They are indeed communicating."

"You're right, Fay. I would never have guessed a garden angel would suggest a chemical fertilizer. It's so against my principles. I have so much to learn about successful vegetable production in Alaska," I sigh. "I need a fast-track education about where to find organic amendments, which to use, and how much to use."

"Looks like we have a busy winter of reading and tune-ins ahead," laughs Fay.

About Supplementing Nutrition

Nitrogen (N) Cole crops and lettuces are called "heavy feeders" because they require a plentiful dose of nitrogen **(N)** to grow their vegetative green parts. Will compost alone supply all the **N** needed to yield the enormous heads expected by shoppers? Probably not. You'll need to supplement the nitrogen provided by compost.

Potassium (K) Potassium is also a major nutrient, serving a multitude of plant functions. Sources include choices like Sul-Po-Mag, greensand, sulfate of potash, and kelp. Potassium may be present in the soil, but not available to plants without proper chemical and biological balancing recommended by your soil test lab.

For more information on soil amendments, please see *Appendix 2* and organic gardening references. **Trace elements** are mostly supplied by applying a liquid fish and seaweed fertilizers, and/or compost, kelp meal, or Azomite.

Fertilizers –
Which to Choose?

MY WINTER SEARCH for organically approved fertilizers plunges me into mysterious waters. I marvel at strange-sounding names as guano, colloidal rock phosphate, Chilean nitrate, Azomite, Langbeinite, Glauconite. Then I read about the granulated "meals" of more apparent origin like fishbone meal, blood meal, bone meal, soybean meal, and cottonseed meal.

Figuring out some of these mystery powders calls for the mentality of a detective. The Inca name for odorous excrement from bats and seabirds has morphed into the Spanish term guano. This bird poop is high in nitrogen and phosphorus. Rock phosphate, a mineral mined mostly from Florida and Tennessee, gets ground up to provide agricultural phosphorus. I learn that colloidal rock phosphate is more finely ground and regular rock phosphate is more coarse. The finer the particles, the more easily the plants can access them.

What's "Azomite?" Some smart guy made up this name for an earthy substance that contains so many trace minerals that it covers plant needs A to Z. Another mined mineral is called Langbeinite but at the feed store, you ask for K-Mag or Sul-Po-Mag. Decoded this way, one can deduce its contents of sulfur, potassium, and magnesium. The amendment Glauconite turns out to be commonly known as greensand. It's an old sea bottom deposit, now found mostly under New Jersey. Glauconite is potassium-rich and yes, it sports a greenish cast.

I plow on through books and catalogs to learn more about these soil amendments. Each has virtues and disadvantages.

Nitrogen is a crucial substance and is sold in various forms. Crops quickly use up nitrogen, and cropped soils almost always need new applications every year. Soil biology will tip the nitrogen toward nitrate or ammonia form. One can choose from sources like blood meal, cottonseed meal, fish meal, and soybean meal to supply this major element. Blood meal's high concentration of nitrogen may burn plants unless applied before transplanting or in low dosages. Blood meal and fishmeal odors may attract bears, dogs, and cats for a couple days. Cottonseed meal comes from the cotton plant so it will not stink, but it naturally acidifies soil. Does my soil need this? Soybean meal most likely will come from a genetically modified crop, and is not organically approved. For phosphates, should I choose bone meal, fishbone meal, or rock phosphate?

Next, I need a source rich in potassium for stem and root development. I have choices like Sul-Po-Mag, kelp meal, and greensand. Crops use up minerals as they grow in the soil, so organic gurus stress the importance of replenishing trace elements as well as the major elements of nitrogen, phosphate and potassium. So my soil will need macronutrients plus micronutrients.

Here my choices get a bit complicated. Sul-Po-Mag is recommended when calcium is plentiful but magnesium and potassium are deficient. Kelp meal contains the most comprehensive array of trace elements that are so pivotal for crop health. But kelp meal applications are restricted to 1lb/100 sq. ft (25g/m²) doses. If I apply kelp meal alone, I'll bet the potassium content will be too sparse. Thus I must choose and supplement with a second form of potash, such as greensand. Such over-choice is getting beyond my ability to guess.

Finally, my references agree that usually the farmer or gardener needs to add calcium (another macronutrient), as well as adjust the pH (soil acidity/alkalinity balance). Lime is the common choice to raise my pH. I learn that, yes, all lime or ground limestone supplies calcium, but all lime is not the same. The experts admonish me to choose deliberately between high calcium lime and dolomite lime.

It all depends on what my soil needs. Yikes! What kinds of nutritional adjusting does my soil need? How do I choose which fertilizers and how much of each? And how do I ensure that I do not over-apply one kind and throw my soil out of balance?

The best way to determine a soil's needs, the experts say, is to send a soil sample to a lab for analysis and recommendations. I don't have a soil test. I did not submit a soil test last fall, and now I am too late. The ground is frozen and I cannot dig a sample. The minute this garden thaws, I'll need to add amendments and plant immediately. I cannot wait two-three weeks for soil test recommendations; my Alaskan growing season leaves no slack. I must calculate and purchase my fertilizers now during my early spring planning period to be ready for May. I will have to figure out something on my own.

Would the Nature Intelligences help me with this? Would the Devas of vegetables and soil prefer one fertilizer source over another? Would they recommend quantities and application rates for me? Since I have no soil test, this is a perfect opportunity to ask the soil itself what it wants.

I boldly initiate a tune-in consultation, asking the Deva of Soil, "What soil amendments do you recommend for the upcoming garden season?"

I feel merriment, but no list of answers. This non-committal topsoil Deva directs a question back to me. *What are your goals? What are you trying to do and grow?*

Oh, right. I suppose you need to know that before you prescribe a scheme. I stumble around with words until I can verbalize my goals.

1. I intend to grow healthy vegetables, herbs, and flowers by organic methods (without certification).

2. I am aiming for high yields so as to:
   a. feed the household throughout the growing season and into winter with vegetable storage methods.
   b. provide surplus to sell for profit and make a partial living.

3. I aim to apply organically-approved amendments in appropriate and balanced amounts, in order to optimize soil nutrition for maximum vegetable production for house and market.

I synchronistically find Machaelle Small Wright's latest book, *The Perelandra Garden Workbook*. This is her curriculum for spiritual gardening, and I latch onto her step-by-step strategy for fertilizer selection.

First, I list the kinds of vegetables, herbs, and flowers I want to grow this year. I map a garden plan that shows each crop's location and amounts. Then I list the amendments I can find at the feed store this year that furnish nitrogen, phosphate, and potassium (NPK):

Nitrogen Sources (N)
- Blood meal
- Fish meal
- Cottonseed meal

Phosphate Sources (P)
- Bone meal
- Fishbone meal
- Rock phosphate

Potassium Sources (K)
- Greensand
- Kelp meal
- Sul-Po-Mag
- Sulfate of potash

I enlist Fay to help me with this tune-in. We sit down with our written list of choices and our pencils ready. According to Wright's method, we simply go down the list one by one and ask the soil and garden's preference about each. We should discern a yes or no. This should give us a customized fertilizer recommendation.

Now then, to whom do we direct our questions? The Garden Deva? Each vegetable? The Deva of Soil? The Over-lighting landscape angel? We settle on the Deva of Soil.

How do we do this tune-in process again? We take a minute to remember what seemed to work best. Ah, yes, remember to approach with humility, respect, and a sense of learning. Hold a precise question in mind, or write it down. Take a few slow breaths, and muffle the volume of our mind-chatter. Deliberately expand loving feelings toward the Being we are addressing. Feel into and connect with the spirit or essence of that Being. Then quietly wait and be open. See what comes to mind. Trust that we will be answered. Expect that each of us will perceive messages in various ways, e.g. sounds, tunes, colors, memories, pictures. Acknowledge and give thanks for whatever we receive. Finally, share and piece together the guidance.

Even if we wonder, "Am I making this up in my mind?" note it without arguing with it. Interpret by thinking about what the symbols and emotions mean for you. Spend some time pooling impressions and interpreting the symbols, imagery, and feelings. Expect answers that carry unconditional love, non-judgment, humor, directness, and non-ego perspectives.

We begin. Not being proficient with the kinesiology method, we use a pendulum plus the confirmation of feeling our intuition to receive the guidance. We are excited to work together, because we can pool our answers. With two or more, we'll get confirmation and more elaboration than we would in attuning alone. We can help each other interpret impressions.

We ask aloud, "Deva of Soil for our garden area, may we please be in conscious connection with you?" (We wait a minute until we feel a connection with a solid, yet playful and happy presence.) "Would you please advise us? We want to partner with you in our garden efforts. To start this season, we would like your help in selecting the fertilizers that best fit the needs of our soil here at Good Earth Gardens. Here are the goals and a list of crops. First of all, do we need to purchase fertilizers, or can we provide enough soil nutrition for the produce with compost or manure alone?"

Deva of Soil: *You need to purchase amendments (supplements). You're growing crops that are heavy nitrogen feeders, and compost or manure alone will not meet the needs. Furthermore, you need a foundational base of minerals for your long-term soil building.*

We give thanks and proceed down the fertilizer list, item by item, starting with organic sources of nitrogen, asking for a yes or no. Then we pool the answers that come into our minds. We both get a sense that the Deva of Soil is delighted by our efforts to ask. We discern a yes for cottonseed meal, bone meal, and greensand. This combination will supply the soil a source for N, P, and K, and some trace elements.

Next we ask the Deva of Soil to advise about the amounts of each amendment to apply, specific to particular beds and crops... "Please give us the application rates in pounds per 100 square feet (9m²)," we ask aloud.

This method is not working! We get numbers ranging from 1 to 20 lbs (0.5 to 10kg). This Deva is playful. We have to close the session, and I have to research the average application rates for each amendment. Then we tune in again, and ask in segments. "From 1-3 lbs (0.5 to 1.36 kg) of cottonseed meal?" and wait to feel a yes or no. "From 4-6 lbs (2 to 3 kg)?" and on up. More often than not, the Deva of Soil tells us to apply more pounds for each amendment than the highest ranges in my main reference book, *How to Grow More Vegetables* by John Jeavons.

We continue, "We really appreciate the recommendations, but they seem so high compared to our references. Why?"

The Deva of Soil: *Ah, you asked how much we would like, not just the minimum we need to get by! This soil is not as effective in holding minerals as other soil types.*

I pour out gratitude to the Deva, and we close this session. This is so helpful. Our tune-in has actually given us a set of customized, personalized recommendations. By listening with our hearts instead of depending on the pendulum alone, we could also "hear" the Deva's cheery personality and feel its warm appreciation for humans who ask for its wisdom.

This is a successful experiment. I love asking the soil directly.

Equipped with a formula, I go buy the fertilizers with confidence, and apply them at the angelically advised rates. I see convincing results throughout the summer, as I observe consistently robust vegetables, no signs of mineral deficiency in the plants, and plentiful yields. We are ecstatic with the full flavor from each of the vegetables we savor at the table, and the freshness they hold long after harvest.

I make this method of selecting fertilizers an annual routine. The next year, the Soil Deva requests fishbone meal to replace bone meal. The year following, the soil requests rock phosphate. We ask why.

Soil Deva: *Because we love the trace elements in the rock phosphate!*

I eventually become more adept at fertilizing various beds selectively, depending on the crop to be planted there. For each bed, I ask for the specific formula for the anticipated vegetable. Red potatoes taught me to apply more potassium in their beds than in those of white potatoes. I had never seen this advice in the reference books.

Another spring has returned to Good Earth Gardens, and this March as I conduct my planning session, I receive no new instructions regarding my nitrogen source, so purchase cottonseed meal as usual. I have a heap of 50-pound (23kg) bags piled in the driveway, all knifed open. Just as I am about to start applying this fertilizer, I am surprised by a news bulletin: Cottonseed meal may be disqualified as an organic amendment.

Oh, oh! Now what?

Fertilizers –
Cotton-Pickin' Residues

INFORMATION ALERT! Information Alert! Information Alert! Cottonseed meal has toxic residues. Organic growers are rejecting this source of nitrogen.

The magazine article snags my attention. My mountain of cottonseed meal bags are poised and ready to spread this week. This soil amendment has virtues of low salt content, affordable price, and it's stocked in a local store. Now this alert details how cotton has probable high levels of pesticide residue. Do I want to keep using this in my organic garden?

I read more about cottonseed meal. This coarse powder comes from the ground-up seeds inside the cotton boll. It is sold for livestock protein and a soil amendment.

The problem is that cotton is classified as non-food agricultural production, so it has become one of the most heavily sprayed crops in the USA. Herbicides, insecticides, and fungicides are all sprayed on cotton fields. Organically grown cottonseed is rare and very expensive (1989). For the moment, current organic certification rules still permit its use.

I begin to wonder. My cottonseed meal is most certainly from non-organic sources. Am I poisoning my precious soil? Will the pesticide residues in the fertilizer be taken up by our vegetables and then will we ingest these toxins when we eat them? Will this amendment harm more than benefit this growing operation? Should I worry? Test for poison levels at a soil lab? Avoid using it? Ignore and hope for the best?

Okay. I want the truth. I want to ask an authority. I don't want government agency opinions. I want an interview with the ultimate expert, the wise soil. I procure my tune-in buddy Fay for extra confirmation, and we connect with the Deva of Soil. We expect a simple yes or no. This does not happen.

Ellen & Fay: Deva of Soil, is cottonseed meal causing a significant problem in Good Earth Garden because of its pesticide residues? Is there a potential build-up of harmful pesticides that negatively affect the soil organisms and/or the humans who eat our vegetables?

Soil Deva: (We do not get a direct answer. We resort to trying a different question.)

Ellen & Fay: Can the Nature Spirits reduce or neutralize the negative effects of the pesticides?

Soil Deva: (Still no clear answer. Try something else.)

Ellen & Fay: Well, what would you prefer as a substitute nitrogen source, e.g. fish meal, fishbone meal, blood meal, or *other*?

Soil Deva: (We get a sense of *other*.)

Ellen & Fay: We're lost. What is it that you recommend?

Soil Deva: *Rather than think in terms of substitutes, focus on attitude and intention. These are vitally important. When you express vibrations of happiness, laughter, care, and blessings, these are as important as a particular soil amendment that you choose to apply.*

Conversely, when one emits an emotion like worry, it gets transmitted right into the soil. Worry does not help anything. Worrying about choosing exactly the "correct" amendment means you are caught up in purist debates and perfectionism.

The truth is, <u>there is no one answer that is perfect</u>. There are slight advantages and disadvantages to each choice of fertilizer. All come close — close enough. All are choices in a positive direction of working <u>with</u> nature.

Ellen: You are telling me that I am trapping myself in a game of "must be perfect, must be right". Aha! I never dreamed of attitude being more important than the fertilizer choice.

Soil Deva: *Please understand that it is far more important to see the larger perspective. Rise above striving for a perfect answer. See that your love and enthusiasm is leading you into organic methods, life-affirming methods. Live it. Sow it.*

You have persisted in asking if there are better alternatives to your fertilizer schemes, so I will make a suggestion. Consider achieving more of your fertility with green manures.

Green manures? From my reading I know that green manures are crops like rye, clover, and buckwheat. These are specifically seeded to mow and immediately plow underground. As the chopped green plants decay in the soil, they replenish organic matter, add nutrients, and feed microorganisms. I haven't done anything with green manure cropping, but you're getting me to think I should. The Soil Deva must be watching me think, and continues: *Green manure is like growing compost in place! These cover crops, living and dead, will hold soil from wind and water erosion and generally imitate nature, which abhors bare ground. But again, whatever methods of fertilization you use, remember the importance of your personal attitudes and energies that you add.*

This sends me delving into more research about green manure or cover crops. Yes, these are crops sown to cut and cultivate right back into the soil. They are not to harvest, eat, or sell. Once under the surface, soil microorganism populations immediately explode and feed on this fresh, tender plant material. Microbes in the soil food web jump on the opportunity to decompose the young cover crop. This creates more humus.

As the microscopic miracle workers recycle these accumulated minerals into the upper topsoil, they also transform the nutrients into forms that are highly available to the new plants to follow. If the green manure crop is a legume, such as a member of the bean, clover, or pea families, bingo! It will actually manufacture significant nitrogen levels — right in place. They do all this for free!

This sounds like a back-saving strategy for me. Green manuring will cycle, re-mineralize, and even produce nutrients, without having to purchase and spread fertilizer. Green manuring replenishes organic matter without the work of turning compost piles and then spreading wheel barrow after wheel barrow. Green manuring will maintain an active level of microbes in my soil, which is certainly my goal.

Glory be! These strategies must be obvious to seasoned farmers, but new to this beginner. I'm just excited that here is a fertility strategy that is simple, low cost, and effective. This will take some planning. It will be tricky to incorporate within our very short growing season. The vegetable crops need every minute of warmth and sun before our soil temperatures drop and not even a green manure crop will germinate and grow.

How might I rotate plots for this purpose, and how much does that put out of production while cover-cropped? Can I sow "living mulches" alongside or even underneath established rows of vegetables? That Deva is stimulating lots of scheming and pondering for me.

Meanwhile, I have to adjust my attitude. It's time to replace my nagging fears with an attitude of appreciation and enjoyment. In fact, I must even allow myself to fail now and then as I experiment with green manures and timing.

Fertilizers – Smear Blood... in This Garden?

Free Blood for Your Farm or Garden

THE STATE'S DIVISION of Agriculture newsletter catches my eye. "This product is excellent to spread on fields and garden soils. Call Mt. McKinley Meat and Sausage Company."

Haul and spread fresh blood onto my garden — from the slaughter of livestock at the meat plant in Palmer? Sounds a bit gruesome. Still, my whole goal is to build soil, not wear it out. So, what's in this free slaughterhouse blood? The Cooperative Extension Agent shows me the mineral analysis. The fresh blood is rich in trace elements like copper, zinc, iron; it also provides high amounts of potassium, calcium and magnesium. These would be highly beneficial.

I was surprised that the analysis did not show 12% nitrogen, since that is the content of nitrogen found in a bag of dried blood meal. Instead, this fresh liquid blood is high in potassium rather than nitrogen. Interesting. Perhaps I could substitute this free blood for my potassium amendment, instead of spending $125 for this year's topping off of potash in the form of bagged greensand (250# for 50 pound weight (23kg). My budget would certainly benefit.

David Wright, a fellow organic grower, enthusiastically endorses blood applications. He pumped slaughterhouse blood on his hayfield using a hose with no nozzle. That was three years ago, and he can still see the evidence of the blood. Distinct bright green lines that received blood vividly contrasted with the shorter duller grasses around them that got none.

David convinces me. I would be recycling a local waste product, too. The director of the slaughterhouse says that the blood is completely safe and disease-free. Just wash my hands afterwards.

I buy a little pump, don my rubber boots and rain suit, and truck over to this blood bank for gardens. The slaughterhouse supplies a bulk tank that they load in my pick up truck. I lug home the smelly red liquid. Thanks to help from my non-squeamish friend Bob Jones, we empty the tank by pump-spraying measured amounts to each bed.

No one else is waiting in line to use this tank, so I continue to haul home load after load. We complete application for one third of the garden on our first day. Since the other soil amendments are already distributed, I rototill the sections that received blood at the end of the day. The smell disappears in a few short hours. I am getting very eager to start planting as soon as this sweaty rain-suit job is completed.

The next morning I look around and stop short. What have I unknowingly added to the garden? Does the blood carry the energies of the slaughterhouse environment? What have I transmitted from their treatment of the livestock, the kill floor and death, and labor provided by prisoners? Have I unloaded residues of negativity here? Is this counter to my spiritual gardening philosophy?

What do the Devas have to say? This is a lucky day, because Jeff Richardson is visiting, and Fay is also home. They both offer to assist.

Let's see, whom do we ask? Do we ask to speak to the blood? To the Deva of Soil? The Over-lighting angel of the garden? Or to God? Aw, shoot, let's invite them all to this conference!

Fay, Jeff & Ellen: Consulting Devas, is the blood from the slaughterhouse beneficial for our use here as fertilizer?

Devas: *Oh, yes. The soil and crops are glad to have it. It completes the circle. The livestock ate the plants growing from the soil. Now those nutrients from the animal can return to the soil again.*

Ellen: Are there negative energy residues in the blood that I could remove?

Devas: *Yes, these are a consideration.*

Ellen: How can I best accomplish this?

Devas: *When you drive the truck into the driveway, do a routine similar to the Perelandra energy cleansing process. This will remove the unwanted energy residue.*

Ellen: Ah, yes, that is the process where I visualize placing a giant filter cloth made of divine consciousness under the truck with the blood tank. Then I ask your help to draw the energetic filter up through the truck to capture all negative energy residue. I imagine lifting the cloth above the aura of the tank, wrap and tie it up, and hand it to God for transformation. Okay, I can do that. Is there anything else I should know, or do, that will help?

Devas: *Yes, as you spread the material, bless each bed. Thank the animals for giving their lives. Thank the cycle of fertility. Keep your intentions and thoughts clear.*

I haul continual loads over the next three days. The deliveries and cleansing processes go well, until, whoops! On this last morning I finish by zealously spraying the blood on raspberry beds, the lawn, a couple of trees, and foundation landscaping before I realize I forgot the energy cleanse for some tank loads. Oh, oh.

Ellen: Deva Team, what do I do now?

Devas: *Picture spreading the filter cloth under your land.*

Ellen: Where I have spread blood, or the entire property?

Devas: *Use the property boundaries, to be all-inclusive, since you can't always remember which batch you spread before doing the energy cleansing.*

Ellen: Ah, yes, that is true. After so many loads, I get mixed up.

Devas: *Leave the cloth under there all day. Gather it up this evening. Ask God to please dispose of the negativity properly.*

This time I make a note to myself to finish the cleanse tonight before bedtime. At last I can sow and transplant into this spruced-up soil. Then I watch as the season progresses. Will this blood prove effective as an organic amendment? As the crops get a footing, I check with them and the Deva of Soil. They report that they love this addition of trace elements and have an adequate supply of potassium. I am pleased. The price is right (free for trucking) and the system of tank pick up is easy enough to continue each spring.

Now if I can just remember to do the cleansing ritual…

Note: Please see Appendix 3 for
Energy Cleansing Process summary.

Fertilizers – Chemical Granules: Should I Use Them?

OOPS! OUCH! Darn it! That is the third time I have tripped over that open bag of chemical fertilizer! I've stored this left-over since working my lawn care jobs in Anchorage. This fertilizer bag contains an 8-32-16* proportion of NPK. Fine. This is the typical kind for general application, and I want to use it up. There's less than one gallon's worth lingering in the bag. It's time I just dump this somewhere.

Where should it go? What area of the lawn, trees, shrubs, or garden would like it most? I tune in to ask.

The answer? I get silence. Actually, I get a complete lack of enthusiasm. That must mean "no". I check areas, one by one. No, from the greenery. No, from lawn. No, from the trees. No, from the garden. No, from the compost piles. No one wants it. Nada. Not even this small bit. No part of the landscape wants anything to do with it.

Why not? It's only this tiny amount!

Not until years later did I learn one main reason. The potassium component of the fertilizer's synthesized NPK (nitrogen-phosphorus-potassium) content is usually muriate of potash. That typically means it is about 50% chloride and 50% potash. The chloride acts like bleach, killing most beneficial microorganisms in the soil's biological food web. These microbes are essential to convert minerals and organic matter into the proper forms and provide this food to the plant roots.

Back at Good Earth Gardens, I am standing here deliberating about how to dispose of this remnant of conventional fertilizer. This is the mainstay of modern agriculture. This is what a plethora of horticultural references recommend for everyone to use. Experts in gardening, farming, landscaping, and lawn care all prescribe these chemical applications regularly. Yet not one plant Deva in the yard nodded yes. These beings say, "No thank you!" unanimously. I wonder what else we humans would not use if nature could vote on it.

Phooey. I give it to my chemical-loving neighbor who buys this stuff regularly anyway.

Note: * (This is a commonly-sold fertilizer formula. The USA label means that bag contains 8% N, 32% P and 16% K.)

Composting:
What about Adding Ash?

SOME PEOPLE LOVE to make bread. I love to make a batch of compost. It is my favorite form of garden recreation. I challenge myself to construct the heap for the hot compost method — so it heats up and cooks down. I get my workout by alternately layering about 1/3 green material to 2/3 brown materials, and water each stratum well. I take the pile's temperature and turn it regularly. I am in constant awe by the pile's transformation into rich, dark brown, finished compost — in six to eight weeks.

Thus I am a dedicated scrounge. I have a reputation as the Compost Queen. I am forever on the lookout for so-called "waste". When I spy a curbside disposal of grass cuttings, leaves, or spoiled hay, I'm like an English Setter alert to fresh bird scent — I come on point. Grab that waste, it will feed my compost piles! Look over there — more potential banquets for the heap. Can I have this discarded office paper by the curb, all shredded? What about adding that raked-up heap of fluffy/woody catkins that the cottonwood trees dropped?

Now then, how about this garbage can full of ashes that I just cleaned from our wood-burning stove? Would ash benefit the compost pile too?

Surely my wood ash contains considerable quantities of minerals. I also understand that ash plus water produces lye — and that means that ash could turn the soil too alkaline. If I add a little ash in my huge compost heaps, would it ultimately help to nourish crops? I want compost to catalyze ideal growing conditions for my vegetables. I want compost to provide as many of the minerals as possible for fertile soil.

So how much ash is appropriate? How much is too much? How can I be certain that I don't cause harm by over-applying the ash and tipping the pH out of balance?

I am stumped. My reference books offer scant help on this puzzle. This calls for another consultation with the final expert, the consciousness of soil.

Again, I recruit Fay. I am gaining confidence in my tune-in abilities, but I love the elaboration and synergy when two or more of us combine efforts. Fay and I invoke the Deva of Soil. This Being always feels very powerful. At the same time, the essence of soil feels close and familiar, like a friend one can always talk with.

We easily establish contact. "Hello, Soil Deva. We seek your wisdom and advice again. What about adding ash to my working compost piles?"

Deva of Soil: *Yes, your wood ash is an excellent mineral booster to your compost piles.*

Fay & Ellen: Great! Will any kind of wood ash do?

Deva of Soil (Fay and I share the impressions we each receive). When we piece them together, the interpretation is roughly: *Be certain you are burning just trees for fuel, not any toxic materials like plastics, trash, batteries, treated wood, multi-colored and glossy paper. This would leave hazardous residue. Plus burning them puts toxic substances into the air we breathe.*

Fay & Ellen: Ah, yes. We do not want to cause air or soil pollution. We are very selective about what kind of paper we burn in our wood stove along with firewood. We refuse to burn trash. Would you please advise us about quantity per pile? We do not want to harm the acid-alkaline balance of the compost pile process. We don't want to impair the final product, or damage soil function or our crops.

Deva of Soil (eagerly and confidently): *The Nature Spirits will be glad to help you. They can distribute and shovel in the correct portions of ash for each new batch of compost.*

Ellen: Nature Spirits? Do you mean those happy but wise "little people"? Those whirling vortices of power described in *The Findhorn Garden* who tend the trees, open flower petals and transfer energies?

Deva of Soil: *Yes, they are here. You haven't been aware of direct interactions with them yet.*

Ellen: Well, I would love to meet them and work with them. How do we do this?

Deva of Soil: *Sprinkle an even layer of ash, not too thick, over the entire pile. Use a little less toward the edges. Coat it like powdered sugar on a donut. The Nature Spirits will work from the top down, shoveling and mixing the ash throughout the whole pile. It's important that Ellie is careful not to apply too* *much ash. Just cover the pile surface, but only with a sprinkling, not thick like frosting.*

Ellen: What do I ask for while I do this?

Deva of Soil: *Invoke the Nature Spirits and me. Lend your energy. Request that this team please incorporate enough ash into the compost pile to add desired minerals without upsetting the soil's pH balance. State that it is your goal to have the pile pH at a level that optimizes vegetable growth in the garden.*

Fay and Ellen: That's all? It's that easy? Wonderful! Thank you so much!

Warning!

If you are passing by when I have finished layering raw material into a new cubic yard (m^3) of organic matter to compost, you may hear me muttering this incantation surreptitiously. I don't want to draw anyone's attention. Then you will see me giggle with joy, because the team dives into the task with such joyful enthusiasm. This work is play to the Nature Spirits, and they love to get creative and joke around as they mix ash throughout the compost pile.

I often see/feel them in my mind's eye, busily stirring the ash into the organic matter with little shovels. Other times I have gotten a sense of them drilling it in with augers, or fluffing the pile with fans so everything re-settles with a proper mix. The whole process takes 3-6 minutes.

I laugh out loud some more, and then I completely forget to muffle my voice when I exclaim, "Thanks, guys! This is terrific! You're wonderful! Blessings all around!"

So watch out for eccentric gardeners like me, cheering and carrying on over the compost pile. Please don't phone the mental health authorities!

Devas and Nature Spirits – Who's Who?

THESE NATURE SPIRITS are so fun. I can see that theirs would be a very useful friendship to cultivate. But who are they, exactly? What is a Deva, and how are they different from Nature Spirits?

The Findhorn Community founders pioneered this process of consulting loving, intelligent essences of nature. Who or what did they contact? They called it some sort of divine consciousness. When speaking with the spiritual entity in charge of a pea variety or species of insect, they called it a *Deva* (DAY-Vah). This Sanskrit term means "a being of light". A Deva is the overlighting angel of a plant, animal, or mineral.

Findhorn founders worked with other energy beings they called Nature Spirits.

Who's who? I want an interview! I decide to put my questions directly to these Beings:

Ellen: How do I explain what a Deva is?

Answer: *We Devas are of the Angelic Kingdom. We focus energy to produce and hold the physical form of something, such as a certain gem or a species of herb or bird. There's one of us per form, each with its conscious energy. Think of us as specific angels delegated to a specific task. Each angel directs the force fields, aligns the mass of molecules, and consciously arranges matter to appear and function as an orchid or caribou, for example. We Devas have different energies and personalities, yet we all reflect the unconditional love and non-condemning essence of the Creator.*

Ellen: I see. Then with whom am I talking when I address a birch tree?

Answer: *You are in contact with a Deva or collective consciousness of that* *species of birch tree. When you contact the Deva of paper birch, you are in connection with all paper birch trees around the world. You are in contact with the accumulated memory, experience, and wisdom of all paper birch individuals, past and present. You can also choose to communicate with an individual tree's spirit as a subset of the Deva of that species.*

Ellen: Okay, thank you for helping me understand. I read that Dorothy Maclean found herself discovering Devas of machines, buildings, landscapes, cities, and nationalities as well. Each has a spirit or consciousness. Each can be contacted. At Perelandra Garden, Machaelle Small Wright expands on this process of working with Devas of projects, organizations, concepts, and even highways. I'm learning that you are not limited to animals, vegetables, and minerals.

So Nature Spirits, who are you?

Answer: *Ah, we are a different aspect of nature. We are of the Elemental Kingdom, and we are evolving just like humans are. We Nature Spirits are the ones who joyfully carry out energy flows, processes, and functions. We direct the energetic processes. Whereas Devas focus energy to hold a form such as a tree, Nature Spirits <u>tend</u> the trees. Devas hold the architectural blueprints; we work out those patterns on physical levels. We are the forces of energy transfer.*

We Nature Spirits oversee the photosynthesis, the opening of flowers, and a multitude of other energy exchanges on various levels. Sometimes we are called Elementals, gnomes, brownies, undines, little people, elves, fairies, leprechauns, and so on. Your artists have depicted us as little men in lederhosen. We Nature Spirits would rather not be limited or confined by thought forms. We emphasize what you learned from Findhorn: think of us as whirling vortices of energy.

Ellen: Yes, thank you! I was riveted to the stories about you Nature Spirits directly appearing to Robert Ogilvie Crombie (called ROC). A dwarf-looking entity named Kurmos visited ROC's home and asked, "Why do you humans collect books, when all knowledge is readily available?" Pan, the great overseer of nature, appeared to ROC as a half-man, half-goat and demanded, "Why do humans fear and persecute me?"

I read how ROC taught Findhorn residents to start collaborating with this extraordinary realm of beings. He said that you Nature Spirits were delighted to be consulted, after so many centuries of being ignored or maligned. Author Marco Pogačnik also writes beautifully about your many facets and great service to the Earth. Is this still true?

Answer: *Yes, we exude joy, wisdom, power, and excellent advice. We are very old and very experienced. Just like the Devas, we Elementals operate in the same unconditional love as the Creator. As Nature Spirits, we operate in hierarchies and chains of command, but never competitively, from ego, or for individual gain. We all work for the good of the whole creation.*

Like the Devas, we will not interfere with or judge human choices. Sometimes we Nature Spirits can be more emotional than Devas. After all, we work so closely to people and the consequences of your choices. Sometimes we feel hostile towards the acts of humans that undermine the good of the whole.

That's what happened at Findhorn when the resident humans ignored their intuitive hesitancy and pruned the flowering gorse anyway. We Nature Spirits went on strike until there was an apology. In some areas, we sadly have had to entirely withdraw our energies where we have been treated with relentless abuse and no appreciation.

Know that nothing makes Nature Spirits happier than to be consulted by humans. When people truly want to co-create harmonious actions with us, we are eager to assist. Keep asking for our assistance. We love to help!

Ellen: Great! Your willingness to cooperate with us humans is truly amazing, in spite of our ignorance and arrogance. You Nature Spirits have certainly assured me of this every time I have contacted you. You have helped me balance the subsoil with a Perelandra Soil Balancing kit. You have worked with me to clean a septic tank. You even neutralized a hazardous substance I accidentally spilled. You are happy, capable, loving, and energetic characters!

I read that some great intuitives (Geoffrey Hodson, Rudolf Steiner, Penny Kelly) have found that some Nature Spirits are young in their knowledge and development, and others are older and much more experienced.

So whom do I invoke with my questions — Deva or Nature Spirits? Or both? Which has jurisdiction over a particular situation? Which do I invite to my tune-in? I'm not always sure I understand the difference between a Deva and a Nature Spirit.

Answer: *Just go ahead and ask your question. We are never insulted by being left out. We are pleased that you ask. You will get an answer from the great interconnected Oneness. Truth is truth, whether it comes from a Deva or Nature Spirits or some combination. We are not rivals or ego-centric. We are just glad to be consulted.*

This is good to know. I remember that Machaelle Small Wright of Perelandra Garden solves this dilemma easily. She simply calls them all **Nature Intelligences**. Nathaniel Altman also finds the definitive lines between

Nature Spirits and Devas quite hazy. In his book, *The Deva Handbook*, he lumps them all into the Deva category. He stresses the importance of simply being receptive to Devic energy or Devic contact, and the wonderful shifts one can experience by this openness and respect.

Thanks again, all of you Devas and Nature Spirits who have gathered for my interview. Blessings to us all and to ever-increasing human efforts to work with you. I close this session with gratitude.

❦

As I digest all this information, I realize that sometimes I feel a need to expand my invitations in the spiritual realm. Then I summon a "supervisor", or call in a whole committee. I'll ask for an overlighting Deva, a landscape angel, Pan, guardian spirits, or the Creator. Often it seems appropriate to invite a group of representatives.

Regardless of proper nomenclature, my tune-ins yield plenty of answers, and plenty of surprises! When people ask, I urge them to simply blurt out their questions and experience the answers personally. Just practice the 3 Cs: Communication, Cooperation, and Co-Creation.

Composting – When is the Pile Truly Done?

MY FELLOW COMPOSTING enthusiast Richard DeBusman puts me on the spot. "Ellie, you've told me that the composting process is finished when:

- the pile turns dark,
- you can't identify any forms of original materials like apple cores or leaves,
- it smells as sweet as the forest floor, and the temperature of the pile is the same as the ambient air.

"But Ellie, my compost looks all cooked at four weeks. Some experts claim that a properly made compost pile will be done at 14 days. Others emphasize waiting two months. That is a big difference. What do you say? And what about introducing worms? What secrets do you know about enhancing those finishing stages? You're the Compost Queen."

"Richard, you have me stumped. These are the perfect questions for Devas and Nature Spirits. Want to tune in right now?" I challenge, happy to slip off his hook. I'm feeling a bit cocky, having logged more attunement hours and gained more proficiency.

"Sure!" says Richard, his eyes twinkling.

Richard and Ellen: Deva of Soil, we would like to ask you about the final stage of making compost.

Deva of Soil: (Conveys a very strong feeling of love and appreciation.) *First of all, think about the effort the human puts into the composting process. What attitudes and efforts (not just ingredients) do you communicate through your* *pitchfork? With you two, you are very enthusiastic. Your emotion of pleasure is an energy and it will recycle into the soil and its nutrients. Second, the more enrichment one puts into the soil by composting, the more rich the harvest taken from the soil. Composting is very reciprocal.*

So, you have questions. It's good to ask. Thank you for caring enough to ask more.

Ellen: We are looking for your wisdom about when a compost heap is actually done and ready to spread on the soil. Some compost experts claim compost is ready after two weeks. Yet a composting expert from Copper Center, Alaska[1] claims one must wait four more weeks <u>after</u> the pile cools down before spreading and using the compost. He claims that nitrogen fixation is continuing to occur. Compost should be allowed to sit and finish processing.

When I instruct people how to do the hot compost process, I tell them to let their pile sit/cure/mature a couple weeks after it has cooled down. Is this true? After cool down, is there a waiting time?

Deva of Soil: *Yes.*

Ellen: How much time is actually needed?

Deva of Soil: *One week minimum, depending on what materials were used in making the pile.*

Ellen: Is the additional maturation time actually for the reasons the author says, i.e. nitrogen fixation?

Deva of Soil: *Actually, you let it sit to become a pile. It is absorbing energy. It is becoming the form of compost, with its accompanying energy. The energies of the raw materials are changing into a new material: compost. If it helps you to visualize what is happening, think about placing a crystal in the center of the heap. It would focus and enhance the process of transition. The heap is still becoming a new product, energetically and physically.*

This is an excellent time to add composting worms (the red wriggler species). They add the final touch. Composting worms do the final stages of refinement: worms process soil minerals into forms most available to plant needs.

Richard: Aha! So we are to provide maturation time and add composting worms.

Deva of Soil: (also speaking for the Creator) *What you are doing when you put forth all that effort to make compost piles is holy. It is parallel to our sacred process of the creation of life. You are using the same methods that we do in nature. Composting is working with nature to recycle and create new life. It is in tune with my love and very important work. All is My Earth.*

I then hear glorious music in my head (specifically, "Now his Glory Hath

Filled all the Earth!" from Mendelssohn's *Elijah*). I break out in goose bumps, as I am deeply touched and very humbled.

"Richard, we have just received a very high compliment. I'll see if I can convey this message I received without getting too teary."

Richard, of course, gets the same heart-touching guidance, and we sit in awed silence for some time… before we start scheming ways to find enormous quantities of red wriggler worms.

---

[1] From the unpublished paper, *"A Brief Synopsis of Composting Process"* by Ted Hesser, Copper Center, AK.

Composting –
To Lime or Not to Lime?

AFTER FIFTEEN YEARS of learning and teaching about composting, certain experts are now issuing a new pronouncement: "You should add lime (ground limestone) to your compost piles." What? All the literature I have ever read says, "Thou Shalt Not."

Why or why not should an agriculturalist incorporate lime into the composting mixture? I do some more research and find that my horticultural references are contradicting each other with, "definitely yes", and "definitely not."

What can I accurately tell my organic gardening class, when the recommendations are contrary?

The books agree that lime provides much-needed calcium. But they also say that lime is like wood ash: it raises the soil pH. So would adding limestone also make the compost too highly alkaline when one applies the finished compost to the soil? Would this adversely affect subsequent crop health?

Bio-Intensive growing expert John Jeavons states, "Do not 'sweeten' the pile with lime. A serious loss of nitrogen will occur." Organic gardening sage Scott Nearing agrees. Yet other authorities such as Dr. Elaine Ingham and Dr. Arden Anderson say their recent experiments show that it is desirable to mix in lime as you build the pile. They claim you want to achieve a higher pH in the finished compost. You want to take advantage of the microbes' concentrated activity to transform calcium into a more available form for plants. They are finding that this is more efficient than applying the lime directly to the soil in the fields. In fact, if you add lime to your compost piles and spread it, you'll actually need significantly less calcium in the soil that receives the compost.

To add or not to add? Who is correct? Can lime help or harm the working compost and the crops? I am mystified. I commandeer Fay to help me ask about this controversy.

As we put this question to the Deva of Soil (DS), we get a sense of deliberations going on behind-the-scenes. Eventually, we hear, *Yes, you could do that.*

Ellen: Your answer seems conditional. What other factors ought we consider?

As we await further communication, I remember some rudiments from my soil studies. All sources of limestone (calcium carbonate) contain calcium and magnesium. Sources vary, though, in the proportions. High-cal lime (or "calcitic lime") has a higher percentage calcium and a lower percentage of magnesium. Dolomitic lime has a higher portion of magnesium. When amending soil, it is very important to know which to add.

Hmmm. My mental wheels begin to turn. Some regions have soils slightly deficient in magnesium; others have plenty of residual. Some crops require more of one or both of these minerals. Heavy agricultural use can deplete both calcium and magnesium.

Ellen: (resumes) So, Deva of Soil, you must be guiding my memory and thinking. Are you suggesting that we have choices about which lime to apply, depending on the status of the soil? Does it make a significant difference?

Deva of Soil: We feel a strong nod of affirmation. *Don't risk over-doing the magnesium levels. It is difficult to correct. Dolomitic limestone contains too much magnesium for some soil types. Be conscious of the two types of lime. Choose limestone to best match your soil's situation.*

Ellen: It sounds like you recommend that the grower send in a soil test. The lab analysis and recommendations will tell the grower about the calcium-magnesium levels. Right?

DS: (We sense another nod of whole-hearted agreement.): Yes, a soil test… or ask me when you hold a sample of each lime and you are in physical contact with your soil.

Fay & Ellen: So first, you recommend that we choose the correct lime. Then how much do we apply to the compost pile?

DS (conveying pictures to me and words to Fay): *As you build the compost heap, apply a light sprinkling of lime every few layers. If you add too much, you could alter the pH too much for optimum growing conditions. In other words, spread it very lightly.*

But it would be so much better if that compost maker would work with us.

Ellen: Do you mean we ask the Nature Spirits to mix it in proportionately? Just like they have done for me with applications of wood ash?

DS: *Yes.*

Ellen: Ah! Let's see if we have this right.

- First, the farmer/gardener needs to find the kind of lime that is most appropriate for his/her particular soil and crop needs.

- Then s/he constructs the entire compost pile.

- Next, the compost-maker dusts only the outside surface of the pile with lime. The dusting should look like powdered sugar on a donut.

- Now, the human asks for help from you, the Deva of Soil, and the Nature Spirits. He/she would specify what pH she would like for the finished compost. (Such as, "Please adjust the pH of this pile to maximize growth and health of garden vegetables.")

- Finally, the composter asks the Nature Spirits to please thoroughly mix in the lime to the proportions needed. While doing so, please expand the quantities of the minerals to benefit crops and to attain the requested pH level.

- The human lends his energy to this process until it seems done.

DS: *That's right! We would be excited to be a working partner in the venture.*

Ellen: I love this! Here we have another cooperative, co-creative venture. Your specific advice is so welcome. Thanks for resolving my dilemma with your wisdom. I am eager to try this method!

Compost Application –
How to Extend my Small Supply?

I IMAGINE myself exactly like a celebrity chef, opening the oven door, ready to spoon a delicious batch of home-made humus into the garden. All last summer I arduously turned and processed raw organic material in compost bins. On this spring day, I feel absolutely rich, gazing over my 2-3 cubic yards (m³)of masterpiece compost. It is cured and smelling sweet.

Today I am poised to begin spreading my pay dirt. What a joy to give such a rich gift back to my soil and the Earth.

I cheerily steer my first wheel barrow load and tip it into the closest garden bed. I watch that heavy load quickly dissipate as I rake it over the first 40'x 3' bed. I screech to a halt. I smack up against the realization that I do not have enough compost to apply it everywhere, to all the beds. I will need at least a half inch everywhere, and that adds up to more cubic yards (m³) than I have for full coverage. I'm looking at a supply of compost that is very scarce compared to the sprawling and needy cultivated areas of the front yard, back yard, and side yard plots. I am stymied. Where to put my iddy biddy treasure?

I default to my dictum, "When in doubt, ask!" So I ask the expert, the angel of soil. I should probably get used to being surprised by Devic answers that I don't read in the common organic gardening literature.

Q: Deva of Soil, I have a limited supply of finished compost. What would be the best strategy for applying it? I assume that I should try to sprinkle a very thin layer of compost everywhere. Or perhaps you can suggest high-priority beds that need it most, while my limited supply lasts.

A: *Actually, I recommend something very different. Apply massive doses in one area. Build the soil in one section of one plot. For example, you could start on the north, one third of Pioneer Plot this year. Then do other sections in succeeding years.*

Q: This sounds like a strategy to bring about a long-term change in the soil, rather than spreading compost thinly as far as it will reach. Is this true?

A: *Yes, we are making recommendations for the long term. This soil is a very fine silt. Its origin is wind-blown dust, called loess, that has settled here. When you add your compost, you make the soil come alive! You're adding microbes and humus to the minerals. The silt becomes full of life. Oh, if you could see the energy rising up from the composted areas as we Devas do! So, yes. Contribute copious quantities of compost to small areas. You will midwife the process of soil becoming truly alive at Good Earth Gardens, one section at a time.*

Q: What plot or plots are most needy of compost right now?

A: *All of the back plots have the most needy soil.*

Q: Would you recommend that I expend all my compost on the back plots?

A: *You could do either of these two recommendations:*

1.) *Spread enough in Pioneer Plot for transplanting strawberries, then the rest onto the back plot where the beans are; or*

2.) *Start composting the north end of Pioneer Plot and do a section thoroughly. Put the back yard plots on a schedule for the second wave next year.*

Q: Ideally, how deep should the application of compost be?

A: *Oh, lots, lots, lots! Ankle deep at least!* (I felt a smile at the exaggerated recommendation.)

Ellen: Thank you very much for this consultation. I will spoon it out as far as my supply goes. Goodbye for now, Deva of Soil. I am heading out to become Santa Claus to the gardens! I guess I'd better keep notes on this scheme each year!

Long-term results

I continued the "massive treatment plan". I progressively dosed section after section over the years. What occurred? In the treated sections, I noticed that the surface of the topsoil no longer developed a crust. In the untreated sections, the frequent irrigating resulted in a crusty mineral deposit from the hard water. Furthermore, I never developed a hardpan layer, though many farms do. I also noticed a springy feeling when I walked on the soil with compost, rather than a packed and lifeless feeling.

These treated soils produced especially abundant and healthy crops. Soil texture and microbial life sharply improved. Plots with compost yielded potatoes with almost no scab; un-composted plots grew scabby potatoes. I presume the composted environment speeded processed nutrients to the plants in easily digestible forms.

High organic matter content from the compost meant more moisture retention. Where sections were rich with homemade humus, I could reduce irrigation significantly; the crops were more drought-proofed. This was most dramatically demonstrated in a place on the lawn where I used to have a compost pile.

When I distributed that heap one May, I sprinkled some grass seed on the spot and I ignored it. The grass grew. I never watered it. In August, following a particularly dry, hot spell lasting several weeks, our whole lawn turned a stressed tan color. Yet that patch, even in its ignored state, remained a deep green. I walked over and I poked my finger into the compost-laden soil there. It was totally dry! Yet there was the grass, living and green!

Compost Application – When to Spread?

AS AUTUMN ARRIVES a year later, I proudly assess my cumulative summer's work. I have several cubic yards (m³) of gorgeous compost at my feet. It's finished and ready to spread. Winter is on its way. If I apply this compost to my empty plots now, I will be a step ahead when the spring rush comes.

I am in the mood to roar around and prepare all the beds right now – in the fall. I become wildly optimistic about getting a jump on next year's soil preparation.

I wonder, though. What happens to compost that sits on the garden all winter? Will melting snow leach away its mineral and microbial richness? Would it be better to wait until spring, just before planting? I want to benefit next year's vegetable growth and health in the most effective way. When would it be best to apply this "black gold"?

I can only speculate; I actually have no idea. Only my garden and soil know for sure. I guess I'll have to brake my exciting momentum, put down my pitchfork, and tune in for advice.

Q: Deva of Soil, what's best for the soil and plants – to apply my compost this fall, or wait until spring? What do you recommend?

Soil Deva: *This particular year, fall application is fine. And your urges to rototill this week are just fine. No problem. Have a great time stirring the compost into the topsoil!*

Ellen: Thank you very much for this consultation. Goodbye for now, Deva of Soil. I'm dashing back to my cart and pitchfork!

The next September, I decide to check again.

This time, the Deva of Soil advises NOT to distribute compost until spring. *Keep your finished compost piles stored and covered for the winter.*

As I write this chapter, I am puzzled. I stop and ask the Deva of Soil, "What would you like readers to know about what season to spread compost?"

Soil Deva: *We emphasize that each person should ASK. And each season is different. Each grower has a varying situation. Simply take a moment to check- in regarding your particular weather, micro-climate, farming methods, soil type, and crops. We are eager to recommend how to make your efforts most effective!*

§

So the Nature Intelligences keep urging us humans to ask, ask, ask before act-ing. Ask alone? Not if I can help it. Yes, I know what the instructors of intu-ition classes and spiritual development workshops say. They all smile and as-sure us, "You should be able to receive your guidance and messages by yourself. You can do this. It is innate. Just practice."

This may be true, but I love the synergy of group tune-ins. I have come to appreciate the beneficial effects of adding at least one other person to the attunement process. A group of two or more raises the amps of reception. I find myself seeking out and actually preferring tune-in buddies to gain a more comprehensive answer. A group provides many advantages: additional infor-mation, confirmation, and elaboration. I like the way this helps me understand the message more thoroughly.

Often I do not get much besides some music when I attune by myself. I used to worry that I was blocking guidance. Perhaps I was deficient or a failure at tune-ins. I have come to realize that group tune-ins not only amplify the answers, they strengthen human cooperation and community. We bond more closely with each other and nature. Now, if I have a choice, I find another per-son before I ask for guidance with an attunement. I love the enriched recep-tion, yes, but I also love what we gain in education about nature's viewpoint and wider human involvement in carrying out nature's recommendations.

Of course, we all have our filters. We have our "hot buttons" and assump-tions. One must choose tune-in buddies who are open-minded. Buddies will need to let go of their own favorite solution or conclusion. They'll need to have a high desire to truly listen to another perspective. The attunement helpers must be dedicated to two-way communication, cooperation, and co-creation for the highest good. As you listen to the resulting information each one shares, you must take into account the individual personalities. Be aware of their frameworks and biases, so you can evaluate and interpret guidance with that appreciation.

I strongly urge you to gather and cultivate good tune-in buddies and keep yourselves "on call" for each other. You need not be face to face; the telephone connection is just fine. Feel into the words of Jesus: "When two or more are gathered in my name there I am among you." You are generating love for the species you attune to. You are generating love for yourselves as co-creators. See what wide-ranging benefits you reap with this combined energy.

Nature Spirit Sanctuary – Dedicating Special Space

WE SEE their loving care and feel them spreading ash energy in compost piles, but where do those teams of joyous Nature Spirits emerge from? Do they return to a certain home? Can they work in spite of our overlay of human thoughts and actions all over this property?

Fay and I decide to ask.

We attune to the local Elementals, and explain, "We have been reading in *The Findhorn Garden* and *The Perelandra Garden Workbook* that you Nature Spirits like to have a sanctuary — a place where you can retreat to and work from. We understand that you prefer it be a place that has no human traffic, and no human energy passing through it. Do you need one and want one?"

Nature Spirits: *We would love to have you designate a sanctuary for us.*

Ellen & Fay: Where would you like it to be? As we ask, we walk around the entire property, looking for suitable locations. We find an area where humans never walk. That northwest corner has an un-mowed and uncultivated area near the road. This patch has many cottonwood saplings, long quack grass (couch), and large spruce and cottonwood trees shelter the west edge. It has a septic field under it, but no one ventures into this area. We ask, "Would you like this "wild area" for yourselves?

Nature Spirits: *Yes, we like this. Please walk the borders of our sanctuary so we all can see exactly the area designated.*

We tramp through the long grass to circumscribe this restricted area. We lovingly hand this 12 x 16 (3.65 x 4.87m) oval-shaped space over as the Nature Spirit Sanctuary, and we make a mental note not to trespass. We close the conversation, and we start assuming that Nature Spirits always need an assigned wild area from which to base operations.

A couple of years later Fay and I visited my cabin in Michigan. This simple structure is surrounded by woods. We asked the Nature Spirits, "Would you like a sanctuary around this place?"

No, they responded. *We appreciate you asking, but we don't need a sanctuary here. There are some bushes we like down by the creek.* They sounded fun-loving and quite content. I marvel at the importance of asking. Nature's answers vary so much with different situations.

Carrots –
The Alaska Timing Dance

I AM COILED tight from my hyper-vigilance! There must be a better way to do this.

Germinating carrot seed is the most tense, challenging, and risky of all my spring planting.

You see, it's a tight contest between our cold spring soil and seed that typically requires 3 weeks and 750 °F (240 °C) for optimal germination. So after I sow the tiny seeds, I cover my gazillion long rows of carrot seed with transparent plastic. The clear sheets make the beds into mini-greenhouses. The collected warmth stimulates germination, but one hot afternoon's sun can quickly fry the tender sprouts.

As I wait for carrot seed to germinate, the days tick by, hurling us right into our June period of hot, dry, and windy weather. Typically, we don't expect rain for at least a month. The soil dries out quickly under the plastic, especially the top quarter inch where the teeny carrot seeds lay.

So every day for 3 weeks I become a nervous vigilante, checking under the clear plastic sheets. Does the soil need more moisture since the sun came out? Yes. I carefully peel back the huge plastic sheets for each bed, apply more water, and anchor the covers down again before the wind carries them away.

As the seeds germinate, I fret again. Are they burning to a crisp while I am at the store?

This tedious management siphons off my precious time while I'm busy getting the rest of my crops planted. If I don't closely tend the carrot beds, I risk losing this whole fragile sowing. I can re-plant, but a later round of carrots will probably not mature beyond pencil size before autumn frost.

Hatching carrot children is stressful. Yet the garden Devas tell me, "Do not worry your seeds into germination!"

A headline grabs me as I thumb through a gardening magazine. **"Plant Your Carrot Seed in the Fall — Get a jump on the planting season!"** Hmm. Exciting! If I could do that, my carrot seed would be in the ground, in prepared soil, all ready to get growing. Seeds could capitalize on the spring moisture before the usual arid conditions set in. I want to ask the Carrot Deva if this scheme would work here. Fay and I tune in.

Fay & Ellen: Carrot Deva, what about planting carrot seed now, just before winter? Would this scheme work at our location in Alaska?

Carrot Deva: *Yes and no. It depends on the weather. The answer is yes, if there is snow this winter, and if there is a warm, early spring. The recommendation is no, if the winter has several thaws and there is much ice and water on the ground.*

Given this year's conditions (people, place, weather) the experiment would yield no germination.

Ellen: Aw gee! The scheme sounded so promising, too. Again, you remind us to keep asking Mother Nature, every time.

The Deva closes with advice that sounds like my mother: *Eat carrots. Carrots are good for you. Carrots make you strong and healthy. Exercise.*

Fay & Ellen: Ha! Well, thanks, carrot consciousness! This must be extra true if it's from you, the Carrot Deva!

Predicting Weather – There's an Inside Track?

"I'M SO EXCITED that I'm bouncing off the ceiling! This is the best idea I've ever heard! Fay, Fay, listen to this! This could be the most significant breakthrough in the whole saga of man and agriculture," I expound.

"Wow! Tell me your earth-shaking discovery!" exclaims Fay, getting swept up in my ecstatic mood.

"Well, we growers are totally dependent upon the season's weather," I explain. "Whole crops are gained or lost because of the whims of frosts, droughts, winds, and floods.

"But...what if we could **predict** the weather? Can you imagine how empowering that would be!?! We could side step disasters. We could choose and time crops – to exactly match the upcoming season's whims!"

"Do you mean we should try to out-guess the professional meteorologists and... *The 1992 Farmers Almanac?*" she queries.

"This is even better! I just read that Machaelle Small Wright actually does this. She asks the Nature Spirits when she ought to plant her Perelandra Garden. One year, the Nature Intelligences told her to wait until late June. She thought it sounded whacky, but she postponed as guided. That May and June, unusually heavy rains flooded the area and washed out the neighbors' gardens. Machaelle started her garden in late June, avoided the problems, and had a bumper crop.

"Isn't that amazing, Fay?! I am hot to try this. Come on, let's tune in! It's so perfect. It's February, just when I do all my planning and timing for the growing season."

Predicting Weather – Volcanic Gardening

WE FEEL GIDDY. This is like planning a party. Fay and I enthusiastically generate the guest list. We want to invite a complete consultation team. We put out the call to the Nature Spirits of the area. Oh, and don't forget the devas of local and bioregional weather, meteorology, climate, and even geology.

We breathe and give ourselves a pep talk. We assert that this is possible. The past and the future are mere illusions, right? We affirm that we can learn what's anticipated for the coming season.

Together, Fay and I ask the consultation team, "What will the 1992 growing season be like in our area?"

Nature Intelligence Team: *For May/June, expect an early spring and increasingly hot and dry conditions. July/August conditions look increasingly cloudy and dark.*

Ellen: It sounds like I can plant spring crops on the normal schedule without a late frost. I got a sense of weather for September being lighter and warmer. Then I saw a picture in my mind's eye of my garden, coated with gray ash.

These gray pictures – do they mean there's a big volcano eruption coming?

Nature Intelligence Team: *Conditions are ripe for volcano eruptions anytime. We don't know when, but they are imminent.*

Fay & Ellen: A few years ago, a nearby volcano eruption produced massive ash. The fallout made breathing difficult and driving impossible. How severe is this eruption likely be?

Nature Team: *Instead of words, they give Fay and I various pictures and impressions. We take a minute to piece them together and interpret.*

Ellen: Does this mean we should expect a big volcano eruption or earthquake? That we should be ready to deal with, or escape, natural disasters?

Nature Intelligence Team: *Always be ready to go, change, or give something up. Expect change, rather than let it surprise you.*

They add in a very loving voice: *Re-think the term you call disaster. You call extreme weather and geologic events "bad". You see these as destructive. You view weather as the capricious tyrant and humans as the victims.*

Instead, recognize the miracles. See how such events stimulate tremendous outpourings of compassion in the world. People put aside differences. They come together and help each other.

❦

Starting in May, I confidently plant on schedule, with frost-free results. June's growing advances well, just as forecasted. On June 27 and again on August 18, Mt. Spurr erupts just across the Cook Inlet from Anchorage. The June eruption blasts a cloud of gas rising 49,000 feet (15,000m) into the atmosphere. The heavy clouds drift over South central Alaska, including Anchorage and the Mat-Su Valley. The eerie gray ash settles on the land, causing airport shutdown, several days of health problems, and massive clean up projects. On August 18, Mt. Spurr blasts again, shooting ash clouds 46,000 feet (14,000m) high. That ash falls and again blankets these areas.

On September 16, the radio announces that Mt. Spurr is shooting another column of volcanic ash. Authorities post an alert: the ash cloud is again drifting this way. What should I do first to be ready? The June and August eruptions (and the pre-season prediction) trained me to anticipate and have a plan. I dash out and madly harvest all the vegetables and herbs I can. I'm a few days early and I am gathering way more than I need for this time. I gratefully finish before the ash comes. Hurrah! The extra storage efforts are worth it — I have avoided the laborious task of washing and rinsing the volcanic powder off each green leaf.

In October, I am so pleased as I look back over the growing season. This prediction technique is just great! We are launching into a new dawn of farming. Wow… spiritual agriculture. I love getting inside information about the weather… and geological events!

I vow to do this every year. But next February I am stunned.

Predicting Weather –
And This Year?

THIS FINE FEBRUARY day marks our first anniversary of Devic Weather Guidance. We are chomping at the bit to receive the Devas' forecast for the 1993 growing season. Fay and I settle down to have another date with the Weather and Geology Deva Consulting Team.

We invite our group to be present and begin.

Dear Nature Intelligences, your last prediction was a fabulous benefit. We're excited to hear your newest directives on the best timing for planting our crops. What's your forecast?

Nature Intelligences: *We actually can't predict.*

Fay & Ellen: We are stunned. What do you mean you <u>don't know?</u> How can you **not** know? You forecasted last year. I look over at Fay. "What could we be doing wrong, Fay? This is the same Perelandra formula that we did last year!"

Fay shakes her head and we ask again.

Nature Intelligences: *It's getting so we really don't know.*

We're baffled. And deeply disappointed. Apparently, all we can do is hope. We hope that we have a great growing season without any major climatic or geological upsets.

We close the session and sit and wonder. Why can't they predict this time?

Predicting Weather – What Is Going On?

"YOU KNOW, I've been hearing more about chaotic weather patterns lately," Fay muses. She shakes off her stunned paralysis faster than I. We are still disoriented. Neither of us feels like jumping up and moving on. That "No Forecast" answer nags like an unsolved mystery. "What do you think, Ellie?"

"You're right, Fay. It's more than news broadcasters sensationalizing the usual droughts, floods, and famines. Bizarre weather does seem to be getting increasingly common and intense. Scientific researchers are starting to connect the dots — the dots between the extreme phenomena and underlying climate changes happening world-wide."

"Do you mean patterns like spreading deserts, atmospheric CO_2 buildup, and the greenhouse effect?" asks Fay. "In our area, old-timers are saying that we have gained two weeks to our growing season, thanks to warmer, earlier springs and prolonged autumns."

"Yes, and ozone holes in the sky, shrinking polar ice caps, and receding glaciers," I chime in. "And what about the massive rainforest destruction? Industrial logging around the globe lays the skin of the Earth bare. Then the sun bakes the exposed ground without the tempering affect of tree canopy. Wouldn't these changes set off different wind and rain patterns?

"In fact, I just read about oceanographers' testimonies in US Senate hearings. They report that entire deep sea currents are changing-even reversing-because of air temperature changes. Warmer waters are moving toward the Poles, bringing in a whole new set of sea organisms with them."

"Humph!" Fay retorts. "Humans are disrupting the whole planet. They are the cause of far more weather changes than they realize. Why are the humans doing such detrimental things to their life support system?"

Fay prompts my thinking. "Well, we are seeing an upwelling of people's environmental awareness. We have gained environmental pollution abatement laws and regulations to reduce destructive practices. New waves of organizations, departments, and councils are springing up in each nation at all levels. Citizens are grouping together to save fisheries, forests, and wildlife habitats.

"Perhaps it would be more fair to say that human activity is affecting the globe in both constructive and destructive ways. People can complacently squander fossil fuel reserves. The inefficiencies and over-consumption spew record-breaking levels of carbon dioxide into the air. Yet people have also recognized the dangers of chlorofluorocarbon or CFC production and are banding together to stop it, world-wide."

Fay keenly sums up our explorative discussion. "The Earth is in constant change. Humans are in constant change. We influence the weather as much as it influences us. When we choose to change, we trigger chains of change throughout the world. People say that the weather can change quickly. Yet we humans can change quickly, too — we can change our minds, change our beliefs, change our behaviors."

"I understand better now," I add. The planet is engaged in a complex climatic tug-of-war. Some people are tearing down the Earth, some are building it up. It's not so surprising that the Devas can't exactly forecast which changes will happen and when. Human influence depends on people exerting free will, and that is not predictable."

This mystery feels much more clarified. It's time for Fay and I to check in with the Nature Intelligences.

Fay & Ellen: Hello again! Is our understanding accurate?

The Team responds: *Yes, you are correct. Earth changes and weather events affect humans. At the same time, humans affect the Earth and weather. Humans can affect the changes either way — more chaos or less extremes.*

All actions add up in the big picture. The big picture is astir with this vast mix of rapid changes and opposing influences.

Just remember that the Earth is a great and caring being, mothering you with nurture. At the same time, Earth lovingly lets you learn the impacts and consequences of your choices about emotions, thoughts, and actions.

And yes, this is why we cannot know exactly what will occur in a few months. Earth changes and human changes are happening so rapidly in all directions.

Fay & Ellen: Is there any horticultural timing advice that you can give?

Nature Intelligences Team: *The best advice we can give you is, Here we come, weather or not! In other words, be ever more present in the 'now' of each day. Try asking us more questions about the short-range future. We can help you figure out what feels right as you approach each phase of the growing season, rather than several months ahead.*

Pruning and Thinning – Controversy and Ignorance

"THIS SIBERIAN PEA definitely needs pruning – it's covering the picture window."

"No! Do not prune that one!"

"Those berry bushes need cutting back to ground level!"

"Stop! That would be way too much!"

"Your landscaping is terribly overgrown and sprawling! It looks like no one lives here!"

"Wait! Leave the greenery alone! I like the shade and windbreak effects!"

"That group of trees should simply be cut down."

"Horrors! There is so much logging on the planet that I cannot partake in cutting a tree."

Welcome to the epicenter of our biggest household disagreement: pruning, felling, and thinning. Since we three friends began caring for the land we had purchased together, we have been discovering that each of us has a different idea of how the yard should look. Jim sees the lilac branches blocking the spectacular view of the mountains. He efficiently grabs the lopping shears and clears the window area of all its woody material. Then Fay comes home. She shudders and sputters. She liked seeing the insides of the lilacs through that window. She loved peering among these branches to watch the song birds up close.

How shall we manage the land with eco-consciousness **and** resolve our human disagreements about pruning our landscaping?

Dying Dogwood - Sacrificed Shrub a Teacher

Jim had cut a red osier dogwood at the base because its growth was getting squeezed out between two other over-sized bushes. The branches were scrawny and only 3 feet (1 m) high. Shortly after Jim returned to his Yupik village school to teach, I found the dogwood top blown off the brush pile. It was shifting restlessly on the lawn. It caught my attention strongly enough to request a tune-in. Fay and I both had a flash of the story of Peter Caddy ordering the gorse to be cut back at the Findhorn Community. He had infuriated the Nature Spirits because he over-rode others' intuitive advice to leave the gorse alone while in bloom. We hoped we had not offended our Nature Spirits. We don't want our land keeping crew to go on strike!

Fay and I asked if something was wrong. It was. The dogwood seemed in agony.

The Red Osier Deva explained, *"When trees and shrubs are killed without warning, they die a very slow and painful death. This is true of destruction by storms and other natural causes as well as by humans. But humans have a choice. They can tell themselves that trees are just things and have no feelings. They can believe that trees are on Earth just for human use. Thus humans can cut and take, take, take. Or, humans can recognize their shared consciousnesss — their true relationship with nature. Humans can work with nature lovingly as cooperators and co-creators. They can inquire and thank."*

We asked the dogwood what we could do for it now. We got only vague feelings as an answer, so we stumbled ahead and improvised. We lavishly thanked the dogwood for its life. We apologized for the human action, which out of ignorance, had caused trauma. We found the stump and blessed it. We blessed the top that was cut off. We placed it on the pile again. We had not known that members of the plant kingdom suffer. We resolved to learn more about warning shrubs and trees, and make extra effort to remember to do it in the future.

Siberian Pea

An energetic friend visits us this November day. Before we knew what was happening, she was outside, diving into a self-appointed pruning project on the Siberian peas (*Caragana arborescens*). They provide the hedge at the front porch, breaking the wind and giving some privacy at the front door. In her pruner's eye, the Siberian pea was a sprawling, unattended embarrassment.

She fixed it for the neglectful residents. Fay, on the other hand, detests pruning of any kind.

In any event, there was no chance to warn the bushes. There lay a huge pile of cut branches. The shrubs, which had been 7-9 (2.1-2.7m) high and wider than outspread arms, were reduced to stumps. The 4 bushes were now woody clumps of 1-2 (2.5-5cm) thick trunks, cut off at the one foot (30cm) level.

Suddenly we have shocked shrubs on our hands. Would they recoup after being cut so low to the ground?

After our dear (and zealous) friend left, we tuned in.

Ellen & Fay: Wow, Siberian peas, we had no idea you would be pruned. What procedure would have been more helpful to you? And what can be done now? You look so severely cut down that we wonder if you can grow back next summer.

Siberian pea deva: *In the future, you can ask us to pull down our energies. This warns us and tells us how to prepare. In the winter part of our life cycle, it doesn't take very long for us to pull down our energies into the trunks and roots. It took maybe 30 minutes to 2 hours.*

The way you ask us to pull down our energies is even more important than the length of time you allow before cutting.

As for this situation, we suggest that you kneel and lovingly stroke your hands down the trunks and out on the soil in the direction of the roots. Ask us Siberian pea shrubs to pull down our energies from the small branches and twigs. State aloud your goal, that you want new growth, young and full, to grow up from the pruned stumps. Look for buds on the stubby remains, and prune just above the highest ones. The buds are where the new shoots will originate.

From the pile of cuttings, find buds on the twigs and pick some off. Rub them onto pruned stumps and along the sides of stumps. Or use a vegetable oil (instead of improvised bud oil) to help the surfaces retain moisture.

Now cover each stump cluster with black plastic bags for further protection. Tie down the plastic bags in place, but not so tightly that you cut off circulation. This will help prevent too much drying from wind and frost. See us happy to reach for the sky, and see our great joy in living.

My fingers nearly frosted doing this task, but I dutifully followed through. The north wind and I had a contest to see if I could wrap and tie the plastic bags around the shrubs faster than the north wind could carry them away. Come next June, vigorous new growth emerged.

Landscaping/Foundation Plantings

Soon I became the zealous pruner — I went after landscape plantings sprawling all over the front of the house. I remembered to warn these trees and shrubs, telling them I would be pruning, and to pull down their energies from the areas I had shown them. I gave them 5 days to do this, and then did extensive cutting back of the spruce, lilac, mountain ash, and crab apple tree. I cut so much that I wanted to check in again.

Ellen: I pruned a lot! Are all of you okay?

Shrub & tree devas: *Thank you for the warnings. We are in touch with you and your intentions. We do not feel slighted or abused.*

Crab Apple

Ellen: Crab apple tree in particular, can you live with some additional pruning right now?

Deva: *I believe so. I am a healthy tree. Being so closely planted to the house is okay, too, just as it would be if I were farther away from the house. Since I am so close, I am quite in touch with the humans in the house. I feel like a part of the household, as well as part of the outdoor world.*

Prune my branches in the following manner. If there is a cluster of branches, cull it down to one. Favor the branches coming out in the direction you want. Go right ahead and start pruning, because you have a clear vision of what you want, and how you want the tree to look. As you start the work, ask to intuitively know what to prune. I will be with you, assisting and guiding.

Red Currants

Four robust red currant bushes grow in our backyard and produce luscious quantities of berries. As soon as the fruit is ripe, we put out the *"Currants Available – You Pick"* sign. We enjoy the income and the customers who come to stock up. A commercial producer of various berries down the street stopped by, and she highly recommended that we prune our currants. She said we would be encouraging more thick berry production at the outer surfaces. More compact but productive growth would occur.

Is this true? Fay and I decide to take advantage of our synergy of tuning in together.

Ellen & Fay: Thank you, beloved currants, for your delicious berries! We sure enjoy you. As for management choices, our goal is to maximize a cash crop, high production of fruit, and easy picking for customers. We wonder how to best take care of you. We've been told by the professionals to prune. Should we?

RC Deva: *I'd rather not be pruned. It's okay if you want to, but I'd rather not.*

Ellen & Fay: Why?

RC: *When our branches are cut off, it is confusing to our flow of energy. It short-circuits our paths of growth.*

Ellen & Fay: Does this mean you lose vigor or productivity due to pruning?

RC: *Productivity of fruit would not be up to the optimum you have experienced so far. But you would still see a good crop. We are excellent bushes. Don't change us unless you really want to. We are strong and vigorous. Those inner berry clusters ripen later, so you have a nice drawn-out harvest.*

Fay and I looked at each other in surprise. Well, that just saved us a lot of work!

Gooseberries

This leads us to attune to the gooseberry bushes.

Ellen & Fay: We read in the gardening magazines about various pruning designs for gooseberries — tall and skinny shapes, round and hollow shapes, etc. We would like to maximize fruit production and not get so pricked with your thorns when we pick your berries in the center of the bush.

GD: *That's the price you pay for us!* (This was conveyed with much grinning and humor.) *We did have a good crop last year, didn't we?*

Ellen & Fay: Yes, you certainly did, bless your heart. What do you have to say about pruning?

GD: *Pruning is okay, but if you decide to prune, start when we are young. Don't prune when we are older. It is detrimental. So decide now. As for the thorns, equate us with the song, "The Rose".* (The last verse came to mind.)

> *Just remember in the winter,*
> *Far beneath the bitter snows*
> *Lies the seed, that with the sun's love*
> *In the spring becomes a rose.*

Ellen: Ah, that is a wonderful way to think about your fruits, not your thorns. What are the advantages of those two patterns of pruning I just saw in a magazine? One was a spreading fountain shape, and the other was tall and narrow.

GD: *Either is fine with me. Choose the shape that fits your needs. Pruning is okay, so long as it is done with a purpose and a plan. Pruning is not beneficial if is it just done haphazardly.*

We enjoy talking to you. We are a happy bunch. We are glad not to hear complaints about our prickers and sour fruits. We like chatting. Fay, have you tried us for tea, as you do with red currants?

Fay: Hmmm, no, I haven't. It sounds interesting to try.

GD: *Ellen, when is your next Gardening with Nature class? We would be glad to be ambassadors for your class. Participants can attune to us for their practice sessions, if you like.*

Ellen: That would be wonderful! I definitely need to prepare questions and solicit appropriate "spokes-Devas" for my course members. Thanks, and thank you for the instructive conversation!

Felling Trees

FAST-GROWING COTTONWOOD trees cause the next round of dilemmas. Cottonwoods (Populus deltoides) invade from the edge of our yard right into the vegetable plots and lawn, and more cottonwood babies spring up from our grand-daddy tree in the middle of the lawn. All these emerging cottonwood youngsters grow about 30 (76cm) a year, spreading roots that aggressively sponge up available soil moisture faster than neighboring spruce and birch roots.

From garden edges, cottonwoods are marching into our vegetable plots in three ways: long-reaching roots, suckers poking up from roots, and thousands of germinating seeds laying on the soil. Encroachment under and into the gardens is advancing faster than we can weed them out. When I start tugging on a trespassing tan-colored root with my garden fork, I pull up an endless underground network of tough ropes. Cottonwoods stimulate my thoughts about getting an ax and a bulldozer. I lick my lips and savor the pleasure of chopping down every bullying cottonwood sapling on every edge.

Our household caused some of the invasion. In the center of our front yard, there stands a monarch cottonwood tree. I cannot completely wrap my arms around its wide girth, and its sprawling branches command striking beauty. This majestic elder cottonwood constantly sends out sucker shoots. As an experiment to have more trees and less lawn to mow, we let some of these baby cottonwoods grow. Three seasons later they peak at eight to ten feet high.

By the time they have reached fifteen feet high, (4.6 m) we realize that we do not want all the saplings. We want to eliminate some that are too close to grand-daddy, and some that obstruct our view. The remaining youngsters could then fill out the area. We also want to prune grand-daddy's drooping branches that slap our faces when we mow under him.

How shall we manage the land with eco-consciousness **and** resolve our human disagreements about pruning our landscaping?

Cottonwood as Counselor

We recently read that scientific instruments can detect screams from plants being harmed. It was definitely not our intention to cause plant trauma. If we could agree on what to cut, could we learn how to cut — consciously? It was time to ask those pesky cottonwoods themselves for direction through our muddle.

Thankfully, we settled on what we want. Jim, Fay, and I came to an agreement: remove all the young cottonwood trees that border on the garden plots. This strategy would favor spruce and birch by eliminating cottonwood's competition for moisture, and eliminate the source of suckers as well. We also agreed to remove some saplings and sagging limbs from granddaddy cottonwood's umbrella.

It did not feel proper to just barge in and start hacking. That would be the same as the plunder of logging all over the planet. We wanted to find out how to avoid another dogwood incident.

We asked the Deva of Cottonwood for advice.

Ellen & Fay: Cottonwood Deva, as a spokesman for all tree species, how can we cut and prune you most harmoniously?

CD: *During the growing season, we would like 4 days warning. We need 2 days to get over the shock, and 2 days to pull down our energies.*

Ellen & Fay: How do we best do this?

CD: *Go to each individual sapling that you intend to cut down. Touch it so it knows that you are addressing it. Thank each tree for its good life and service. Tell the tree what you intend to do and why. Then ask it to pull down its energies into the earth. Since the whole tree will be sacrificed, ask the tree if it would please donate its energies to a nearby tree. Specify the neighbor tree you would like to receive the transferred energies.*

Explain that you will wait 4 days to cut. Then when you come back to cut, do so with assurance. You have given appreciation. Your advance notice has helped the tree to minimize shock. Your suggestion to transfer energies to another tree helps too. Designating a donation is something we cannot do, but you can, since you are humans and have your free will.

Ellen & Fay: What if we cannot cut exactly after 4 days? What if we get diverted with something?

CD: *You can still do it within 7 days instead of 4. After that, it is too difficult for the trees to hold down their energies. Here's where you'll need to do some planning. Check your calendar, or perhaps mark your calendar, so you can keep your promised date of return.*

Ellen: Yes, this does take considerable forethought. When I get the time and I get in the mood, I just want to charge outside with my saw and ax and start cutting. Now I must stop, define exactly what I want to do, and then go talk with the trees. After all this, I have to stop action for several days. I have to make sure I can keep my date with the trees.

What methods do you recommend for pruning branches, rather than chopping down a whole tree?

CD: *You'll need to be specific about what you plan to prune. Mark the branches. Ask the tree or shrub to pull its energies down below that cut line. Then wait the same 4 to 7 days.*

Ellen: How do I mark the intended cut lines?

CD: *You can do it in a variety of ways. Mark with pieces of bright string, or crayon, or surveyor's tape. You can simply put your hand on the intended cutting spots, but you'll have a difficult time remembering each place when you come back in a few days. If you are giving a thick shrub a haircut, show it the general line or level you are aiming for. Touch a few branches in the intended line across, and wave your hand back and forth along the entire cut line or shape. Explain that you'll be pruning everything to that height.*

This, I discovered, was tedious preparation. I had to think through what to cut, rather than dive in with saw, ax, and loppers. When I finally began the pruning and cutting of the cottonwoods, I did so with some anxiety. Was I still causing some pain or trauma? I asked, "Is this okay for you?" I was overcome with the answer. I felt great waves of love and gratitude for being so considerate of them. Enveloped in that peace, I continued, enjoying the timelessness. It was a fun workout, but not work.

The next day, Fay and I asked the Deva, "Whew! That took a lot of extra planning and marking. Does all this procedure actually make a difference? What was it like for you?"

CD: *Oh, yes, yes, yes! More than you will ever know. We wish that we could adequately express how much you helped. It helps significantly, and the ripples from your loving actions continue to spread beyond your property.*

Onions – Round 1:
Creepy Crawlies In The Bulbs

"DO YOU have onions?" a customer asks one Friday afternoon in my market garden.

"Hmm, it's July 27. I probably have a few mature enough by now," I offer, and head to the onion patch.

I expectantly pull one. The bulb is black. I pluck another onion, and then another. Each bulb is discolored and rotting. The flesh reeks. How about the next bed? Same thing. I hurriedly spot-check throughout my 5 beds of onions. Each bed is 50 foot (15.4 m) long, with two rows of onions planted per bed. I find heavy infection rampant everywhere.

The customer waits and wonders. I quit my frantic search and tell him that I'm sorry, I don't have any onions available after all. May I help him with some other vegetables?

He leaves and I stand over the onions again. Is my whole crop ruined? By this time in late July, the bulbs should be getting big enough to cook with. I pull a few more. I find only stunted roots. The once-firm white bulbs are squishy and distorted. A stench of decay emanates from the once-healthy flesh.

I peer closely to inspect. Seething and squirming, little white "worms" emerge from the blackened bulb. My stomach turns queasy. And every onion bed is infested. I can almost hear the larvae saying, "Hey, who is disturbing us out there? Where's all the light coming from? We were working at our purpose, which is gorging on tender young bulbs of the onion family."

So this is the culprit: onion root maggots! I dig through my garden pest books and learn that this species is attracted to members of the onion family; it's a different species than the turnip root maggot. The life cycles are very similar. I talk to old-timers in the Matanuska Valley. They never used to have onion root maggots as a pest. This critter is a recent immigrant to South-Central Alaska.

Is this menace devouring my leeks and chives, too? Exasperated, I shake my fist at this pest. I look like I'm in a scene from *Gone with the Wind* when Scarlet O'Hara thrusts carrots into the air and makes "As God is my witness…" vows. I had better cool down if I want to ask this Deva for cooperation. I take a short walk and then ask Fay's calm help.

Fortunately she is available for a team tune-in. I breathe and talk myself into conversing.

Ellen: Angel of these onion root maggots, your form is all over the place, and you are taking way too many onions! Can't you just go away? There are too many of you, and you are destroying my whole stand of onions! This crop is one of my sources of income in this market garden. We also plan on a household supply of onions to store for the winter. I see your destruction everywhere. Yuck!

Onion Root Maggot Deva (sounding unflappable in spite of my accusative attack): *You've provided us with onion heaven and you want us to leave? Talk to us earlier next year. Imagine the situation from our perspective. All we see are onions, onions, and nothing else. You have heaped up the soil with our food, in every direction we turn. Delicious, too!*

Ellen: I soften as I hear the deva speak without defensiveness or anger. What do you recommend?

ORMD: *Try mixing your onions among other crops next time. Right now, you could interplant marigolds in between your double rows of onions in each bed.*

Meanwhile, have people look at us! We are wonderful! Birds happily eat us. Beetles love to eat us! Show us off! We embody a marvelous form!

We close the connection and I mull over the maggot's message for some time. I realize that I am not ready to give up on the whole onion crop. I must say **something**. What recourse do I have? I will need to go back to this deva to find out.

Onions – Round 2

ON JULY 28, I march out to the garden and attune again to the Deva of Onion Root Maggots. I hammer home four points.

Ellen: Hello again, Onion Root Maggot Deva. I've simmered down, and I have thought about what you said. Here's how I feel.

First, I know clearly what I want. I want cooperation with you. I serve as the keeper of the garden, and I have much to learn from its creatures and components, like you! I define keeper as the one doing the planning and implementing, but also the one who listens and cooperates.

Second, I am asking for my fair share. I believe this is a legitimate, reasonable request. I do need a good market crop and winter supply of onions to store, and onions are a main part of my livelihood. I strongly ask you to please come up with a plan that leaves me with the remainder of the non-infected onions. I will work with you and do my part of the plan.

Third, I acknowledge that you have already established your high numbers of hungry larvae. I appreciate your natural programming to feed on the huge onion supply in this garden. You are simply doing what you were created by the Creator to do. It feels good to know I can talk to you with respect and harbor no resentment. We can both operate from a place of honesty. I trust that you will tell me what you can and cannot achieve.

So, now you know what is on my mind. I want to listen to you with an open mind and an open heart. Tell me what you want me to know.

I hear no message in words from the onion maggot deva.

Instead, I experience strong pulls on my heart, viscera, and solar plexus. It feels like a deep, deep yearning or soul connection. It is not unpleasant, but so powerful that I am not comfortable. I want to find the control knob that turns down the volume. How much longer can I handle this heart grab, this pulsing energy in my chest?

I am keenly aware of a loving presence caressing me and beaming love at me. I weather wave after wave of goose bumps. (I often get goose bumps when I connect with truth and love.) I am deeply touched. I feel very cared about. How can this be? I am a representative of **humans**... the ones who have cursed, abused, and persecuted the Earth and the onion root maggot. Could this wonderful outpouring of love come from the deva of this hated pest?

Tears stream down my face. I sense relief, too. This deva is not sending me blame, disgust, or animosity. I am not hearing, "Tough luck, gardener, but it's too late to save your onion crop." I feel forgiven, or actually unconditional acceptance. I sense only love and appreciation. I linger and soak in this nearly overwhelming gift.

Eventually, I take a deep breath. I quietly restate my desire to work out a scheme, and ask that we communicate again soon when Fay can assist me. I give thanks as best I can express, and disconnect with the Deva. I drive off to do an errand.

Onions – Round 3

AS I MOTOR into the driveway, I notice three magpies scattered around the onion plot. I watch them peck at the plants. I hustle over to see the plants they pecked. These are the blackened and yellowed onion sets, but they are intact. The ground around the bases, however, is disturbed. I pull up some of these disturbed onions, expecting to see the root tissue filled with the usual larvae picnic. None! Can a bird get down under the bulb, where the maggots live?

I check under onions without magpie disturbance. That one has maggots, and that one, and that... Oh! A centipede scoots out of the hole and startles me. This onion has no maggots. Hmm. Centipedes generally eat other tiny bugs. Has this one been eating maggots?

I well up with wonder and tears. I plop down on the warm soil beside the onions. The thought strikes: I'm being shown that the magpies and centipedes are maggot predators. Could this be a stage and the actors are communicating to me? The Deva must be orchestrating this nature documentary to show how onion root maggots feed other life in the local web of life. I sense an even bigger miracle. The Deva is showing me that its cooperative scheme is already in progress. Yes, this is what it feels like. I am awed at receiving these loving gifts. This is communion, not just communication.

I bask in this miracle. It is a long time before I collect myself and go inside.

Onions – Round 4

THAT EVENING, I update Fay about the Devic drama in the onion patch. "I've just been given a personal staging of Food Web Theatre," I recount. "Furthermore, the crop infestation is prodding me to recognize my own needs. I am learning that it took enormous courage for me to muster up the assertion, 'This is what *I* want. You already have your share.'"

I describe as best I can how the deva bathed me in love as a reply to my plucky demands for a cooperative plan. Finally I learn what it feels like to be so interconnected to all species with the bond of love.

"Fay, would you please help me tune in again? I'm ready to see what else the Onion Root Maggot Deva has in store." We open the session.

I speak for both of us, saying "Deva of Onion Root Maggots, thanks for your love and your dramatized lesson! What plan have you designed for us to carry out together?"

Onion Root Maggot Deva (transmits different things to us.) Fay hears the moving song in her head called "O, Mystery". It's from musician Paul Winter's mass *Misa Gaia*. The message is to *feel the Mystery (the loving Creator) in us, in the maggots, in everything.*

The Deva shows me a sequence of pictures:
1. I see a colorful fly that represents the adult form of the onion root maggot. It beats its wings, slowly at first, then faster.
2. The fly lifts off from the ground between the onion rows.
3. I watch myself catching this flying insect in mid-air, and rubbing some stuff on its eyes.

4. A hand appears. It has prisms for finger tips. I see it wave hello. Then it vigorously digs up onions one by one and eats all the maggots in them.
5. Then I see myself planting the tiny onion sets in bare soil, as I did this spring.
6. I behold the onion sets growing into mature onions with large bulbs and tall tops.
7. Finally, I see stage lights and spotlights beaming on a celebrity while crowds cheer wildly.

We ask for some help to interpret the meaning. We learn that the Deva is willing to far surpass just working with me. The onion root maggots are creating a special magical solution to benefit me. "The stuff on the eyes" means that the adults who are ready to lay eggs will be blinded from finding the onion section of the garden. That means that no new larvae will hatch and become established. The Deva will systematically remove larvae from each onion (with prism fingers).

The onions will fully recover from maggot damage and mature into healthy cooking onions. Much like the symbol of replanting onion sets, the crop gets a fresh start.

The scene of cheering and spotlights is the Deva's way of saying, "And then I will become a big hero!" This Deva has a mischievous and light-hearted sense of humor. **Wow!**

Joy and humility flood over me. For the first time, I realize that I truly do love to have these beings in my garden. I had a glimpse of this gratitude when I was working with Charlie, the turnip root maggot. Now I feel a blast of love and appreciation for the divinity of all the creatures, even in maggots that eat my crop! These organisms that I have been calling pests are part of the natural community. Their spirits are so extremely loving. Furthermore, they are humorous, truthful, helpful, and communicative! In many ways, the Devas are easier to deal with than many people.

On July 29, I still see plenty of larvae as I harvest some onions for a customer. Ah ha! This process will take some time. On August 2, I return from the onion patch. All the onions are very strong, vigorous, and healthy. I cannot find any wilting or any maggots. On September 21, I am wide-eyed. Miraculous! I harvest ample onions for the customers that want them, and bring in a robust supply to store for the winter.

My utmost gratitude to you, Onion Root Maggot Deva!

Onions –
What about You?

I SUDDENLY WINCE with a realization, and run to find Fay for an attunement. Fay supports while I blurt out my supplication to the Deva of Onions. Omigosh, Onion Deva, we've been ignoring you! We have been chattering constantly with the Onion Root Maggot Deva. Our focus has been on the problems of crop damage. We have been talking **about** you, but not **to** you. Whoops! We'd better stop and introduce ourselves. It's time we converse directly with you, personally.

So hello, and thank you for growing here. Just how are you doing?

Onion Deva (in a strong and cheerful tone): *We are radiating our energies and fulfilling our magnificent stages of life and growth. We enjoy your garden. We do not resent being eaten by other life forms, be they root maggots or humans.*

Fay & Ellen: Well, thanks for interacting with us. By the way, do you have enough space between plants?

OD: *The spacing between plants is fine. You can repeat that next year. We could use more potassium incorporated in our plots.*

Ellen: Okay, thanks. I will apply more potash. Anything else you need?

OD: *We strongly urge you to inter-plant flowers amid the onion plants.*

Fay: Do you recommend a specific kind of flower?

OD: *No, just be sure to plant ones that blossom in lots of different colors. Choose kinds that remain short at maturity, so they don't shade the onion greens. Also plant other vegetables among the onions.*

Fay & Ellen: Okay, and thanks again. We appreciate you and your tasty form. What would cooking and meals be without you onions!

I wonder if I can remember all this information come the bustle of next spring. Thirty-five crops will be competing for my attention.

Onions – Round 5

I GRIT my teeth. I force myself out of procrastination and onto my hands and knees. I crawl around among garden beds that look like knee-high-covered wagons from the Old American West. I must peel back fabric-covered tunnels to check onion progress, invisible underneath.

"This is a blind way to garden," I mutter. "It's no wonder I am reluctant to check progress under these wire arches and white cloth coverings. I'm rushed and it's always easier to inspect my uncovered crops than these things."

Still, I'm proud of my newly acquired spun-polyester row covers. The catalogs rave about how effectively they keep out pests. It's a non-chemical solution and a deterrent that's organically approved. After four years of simply not planting onions, this row cover fabric gives me a new tool and new hope. I gingerly dig up cloth sides I anchored in soil, and peer inside the miniature Conestoga wagon beds to see what is happening to this year's onions.

What the heck? This cannot be true! I'm seeing wilting and yellowed onion stems all over the place. I pull a few and examine. Oh, oh. Each has rotting bulbs squirming with my old friends, the onion root maggots.

I glance around nervously and try to think. I planted **11 pounds (4.9kg)** of onion sets here. I have laboriously planted them and tediously weeded them. It's late June now, and too late to replant.

Rats! My new barriers are supposed to work. That's why I bought yards and yards of these floating row covers this year. The polyester fabric is designed to be a season extender, frost protection, AND screen out those darned flying adults trying to lay eggs on my crops. I was so confident in this product that I planted all the onions together. I had to consolidate, so that I could encase the beds with this fabric. Now I realize I have another serious infestation of onion root maggots! Do I have a totally ruined crop?

I can think of no remedies. The only option left is to humbly connect with the Deva of Onion Root Maggots... again.

Ellen: Onion Root Maggot Deva, I am astounded at the high population of maggots in the onions, in spite of my row covers. What happened?

Onion Root Maggot Deva: *The row covers prevented a percentage of influx, but did not stop all the adults from finding a way through or underneath the loose-woven fabric. Those adult flies are persistent! Actually, the row covers did not stop any more onion damage than good old interplanting would have prevented.*

Ellen: I see. I'm concerned about losing the whole onion crop. What can we do about this?

ORMD: It's too late to stop anything this year. Talk to us next year.

Ellen: It is unacceptable to me to take a total loss. It's also unacceptable to me to wait until next year. Onion Root Maggot Deva, let's get creative! I want to work out an agreement with you so that I can harvest some onions this season. What would you propose?

ORMD: Perhaps there are two strategies — one for this season and one for next year. For this year, it is too late to reverse the damage done. I recommend a thorough cleaning out of infested onions.

Ellen: How?

ORMD: *Dig up all the infested onions from the beds. Dig at least 6" (15cm) below any roots, and 6" (15cm) beyond the row. In fact, get rid of your chive plants in the herb garden, too. They are harboring larvae that will mature and re-colonize your other Allium crops.*

The idea is to start over with new, clean plants, and remove all larvae that could over-winter. It is best to do it now, rather than wait until the end of the season, when our population will have grown considerably.

Ellen: Do you mean dig under the sickly onion stems, remove the onions and soil underneath, and try not to disturb the healthy ones?

ORMD: *Yes.*

Ellen: Whew! That is a huge digging assignment. Where should I take that large volume of soil and maggot-filled onions?

ORMD: *Take it to the dump, or FAR away. You could even take it to a lake. The fish can eat the maggots.*

Ellen: I would still like to earnestly request that you only take 5% of this crop.

ORMD: *Even after your dig-'em-up project, we'd better say 10%. We will try to maintain a balanced population so as not to devour your whole crop. It will be good to have a fresh start, if you can follow through on the digging and disposing.*

Ellen: What about next year?

ORMD: As the gardener, talk with us onion root maggots in February. While you are doing your garden planning, include a consultation with us. Contact us when you have decided what you want to plant, and where, and how much.

Ellen: What else can I do?

ORMD: Again, we recommend interplanting onions all over the garden, here and there. Otherwise you'll give us free dining in Onion Heaven again.

Ellen: What about using those polyester row covers?

ORMD: *Try both methods. Plant some onion sets all together in beds under row covers, and seal them down better. Plant other onions without row covers, but inter-mix them among different crops. Also install row covers on your new and un-infested chive plants.*

Ellen: And of course, I should continue the practice of crop rotation.

ORMD: *Yes, always plant onions where you have not grown them the previous year.*

Ellen: Well, thank you, onion root maggot deva. I will do my best to carry out all your recommendations. You know, I've just realized that we have talked extensively, and I have not asked your name! Do you have another name besides "Onion Root Maggot Deva?" What do you like to be called?

ORMD: *"Onion Root Maggot Deva" is fine. Treat us like you would treat your best friend.*

Ellen: Thanks! I so appreciate your coaching and your generosity with me. You are helping me undo my attitude of "hate the pests" and other thoughts that provoke warfare! I am very encouraged about planning with you in February. See you then!

I carry out the dig-and-dispose recommendation. I lug out a tremendous amount of soil and rotting onions over the next few days! In September I eventually harvest some very nice mature onions, so the control measures did help. I reap enough onions for the household, but not enough to sell. I am just grateful not to lose the entire crop.

Ah, but come February, I will learn some new and wondrous scheme. I can hardly wait to enact the Deva's plan and enjoy a huge and maggot-free onion crop next summer.

About Floating Row Covers

The thin fabric is made of a spun polyester fabric, similar to the lining on the underside of a couch. These lightweight cloth coverings provide an insect barrier when sealed over beds of crops. The row covers let in light and water, but screen out adult flies looking for host plants on which to lay eggs. Row covers also provide frost protection from 1 to 6 degrees below freezing. Row covers are now common in the gardening catalogs under brand names like Reemay, Agribon, etc. They come in different weights and strengths for season extension. If used carefully, they can be re-used another year.

Onions – Round 6

YIPPEE! IT'S FEBRUARY! It's time for my long-anticipated appointment with the Deva of Onion Root Maggots.

I eagerly gather up my garden planning papers and my reliable tune-in companion, Fay. I settle down for a productive planning session with the onion root maggots. I'm as excited as a kid at Christmas. I'm ready for the grand unveiling! The deva will propose a grand new system – a way to harvest more onions with dramatically less maggot damage. What it will be? A particular trap crop? Some predator insect that I will release? Wood ash treatments?

We open the session, connect, and request the recommendations from this high spiritual source.

The Onion Root Maggot Deva just groans and asks, *"Gosh, do you really feel that you need to grow your onions? They are so susceptible to infestations. You could try daffodils as a trap crop, maybe. But would you consider just buying onions? Onions are not that expensive, and then you'd have more space for other crops. I'm just not that optimistic about being able to promise you a large, uninfected crop."*

Do I hear this correctly? Is this all? That I would do well to give up my goal of growing massive quantities of home-grown organic onions? I argue. I try asking in other ways. Fay confirms the message: forget raising onions as a crop. The efforts just won't generate the results I want. I look down at my garden planning map. My mind spins. I need a day or two to revise my optimistic momentum.

The Deva of Onion Root Maggots eventually convinces me. But as spring soils thaw, I cannot resist sowing a household quantity of onions. This time I plant my 1 pound (instead of 11 pounds, (4.9kg) of onion sets "in disguise". I scatter them here and there, tucked in amongst savory, celery, and beets.

Come September, after I remove all the vegetable residue, I discover once-hidden and long-forgotten onions. How do they look? I gaze at impressively enlarged, healthy, and impeccable onions. I see NO root maggots.

I ask other vegetable growers in the Mat Valley. They tell me that the onion root maggot has been practically non-existent for them this season, too. We speculate that severe conditions in March and April probably killed back this species' population. Perhaps this was the **one** summer I could have successfully raised gigantic onion crops after all.

It appears that even my consultant, the Root Maggot Deva, cannot always accurately predict the many variables from season to season. It also appears that I have been very slow and stubborn in learning the lesson of inter-planting. This Deva patiently proved it to me.

Truly, when a grower inter-mixes and inter-plants a variety of flowers, herbs, and vegetables in the same bed, s/he imitates the wisdom of natural ecosystems. Diversity effectively confuses pests, minimizes spread of disease and pest damage, and maximizes beauty of color, texture, and aroma.

The Terms: Monoculture, Companion Planting and Inter-planting

Monoculture: planting a single variety of a crop in one bed or in one field. Monocropping makes it easy for a pest to find its favorite food target and go from plant to plant without difficulty.

Companion planting: planting compatible species together in a mix, as the chemistry of each enhances the others' growth. For example, onions thrive well next to beets, strawberries, tomatoes, lettuce, and summer savory. They do not do well next to beans and peas.

Inter-planting: planting a mix of flowers, vegetable varieties, and herbs together. This deters pests from finding preferred hosts, and from being able to munch down the row of monocrop, uninterrupted. For example, when planting the onion family, inter-plant with sage, and other herbs, flowers, and vegetables. Place the onion members throughout the garden rather than all in one bed.

For more pest management options, please see Appendix 1

Mother Teaches Prevention – Managing Pests, Weeds and Disease

MOTHER NATURE is slowly but surely schooling me. This garden is my training ground. I'm learning what to expect. Given enough experience, reference books, horticultural experts, other gardeners, and tune-ins, I might just learn to skip the emotional speed bumps of frustration, self-pity, and feeling affronted when invasions strike. I can expect that:

- Prevention is the best strategy.

- Even then, pests can appear, and pest populations can skyrocket quickly. Their numbers often peak during that critical time when transplants and seedlings are adolescents. When I start to see damage, I know I will see a lot more soon.

- Each growing season seems to favor a different predominant pest.

- When disease and pests appear, they are messengers. Nature is sending me a message. The message is, "Ellen! Your garden's growing conditions are encouraging us. There are factors that are attracting and promoting our proliferation. The situation is fostering our population explosion. Something is out of balance in our favor. Some factors are within your control. Be a detective and look around."

Yes, dear Nature Spirits and Devic Coaches, I am learning to build in prevention strategies to my gardening regimen, such as:

1. Start with the soil. Make certain that it has adequate organic matter, moisture, a healthy soil food web, and a wide and balanced supply of mineral resources. Keep testing and amending every 1-2 years to maintain soil fertility and mineral balance.

2. Choose varieties appropriate for my microclimate and bioregion. The more I try to grow greenery that thrives in USDA Hardiness Zones warmer than mine, the harder I will have to work. Attempting to raise tomatoes, corn, and peppers outdoors in Alaska requires lots of extra fuss, supplementary heat, monitoring, plastic, and coddling. A determined gardener can probably grow any plant species, if s/he is willing to provide the proper shelters, temperatures, wind barriers, and moisture levels to overcome the climatic stress. How much effort and expense am I willing to expend?

3. Rotate crops. Don't plant the same family of plants in the same beds a second year, or the pests will be ready and waiting.

4. Inter-plant or mix a variety of flowers, herbs, and vegetables next to each other. Avoid monoculture (a single variety per bed). Ideally, utilize companion plants. This diversity confuses the pests trying to target the right host.

5. If I sow a monocrop, use a barrier or sprays that deter the pest from gorging right on down the row. Polyester row covers work as a barrier if meticulously sealed down. Pest sprays include soap, garlic, pepper, etc.

6. Monitor and anticipate. Yellow and blue sticky traps will tell me what insect pests are beginning to get a foothold. I need to be ready to release beneficial predator insects quickly when traps indicate a potential pest problem.

7. Plant a bit more than I actually need. If I deliberately plant an extra 10% for my fellow species, I can relax and let them enjoy some of the yield. I always seem to have plenty for human consumption.

The folk adage about planting is still true:

> *One for the blackbird*
> *One for the crow*
> *One for the cutworm*
> *And one to grow.*

8. In short, don't create a garden that will invite problems. Do the prevention strategies to ensure plentiful harvests even when unexpected pest and disease outbreaks occur.

9. Finally, don't forget to communicate, cooperate, and co-create with the life forms in and around the garden. Loving diplomacy is so much more satisfying than angry warfare.

Lettuce –
I've Been Slimed!

I'M A PROUD momma. My babies are my lettuces. I've known them since they hatched from seeds in 6-Paks. My kids have put down roots now, deeper and deeper into the garden homes I prepared for them. I enjoy watching them spreading their leaves and forming a canopy over their beds of once-bare soil. They fill in this earthy canvas with vibrant shades of lime, forest green, burgundy, and magenta.

What a great pleasure to be husbanding this riot of varieties: head lettuces, leaf lettuces, bibb and butterheads, and Romaine or Cos lettuces. I am especially looking forward to harvesting the red Romaine. I had never tried this variety before, but red looks as stunning and promising here in the garden as it did in the seed catalog.

As I survey the maturing process this morning, I am astonished. These plants have doubled in size in a couple of days! Alaska's long summer daylight drives a frenzied rate of growth. Some of my children are big enough to harvest.

I grab my knife and bound over to the patch with my newest trial variety, the red Romaine lettuce. I aim, cut, and pick up this leafy scarlet bouquet to admire. Then I spot an outer fringe of dead tissue. I look closer.

No! This can't be! Is this the only one? I scan the rest of this bed. I see that almost every head flaunts this horizontal striped edge. I slice open the head. Eooou, the inside squishes. The core — that should be crisp — reveals limp, pale, watery leaves.

Is this is what they call "tip burn" and "slime"? No customer of mine wants this Romaine, no matter how gorgeous the outside bouquet. The poor buyer would take it out of the refrigerator for salad, only to discover the center is a slimy rotten mess.

Hmmm. What's the status of the iceberg and butterhead varieties in the next beds? These appear healthy on the outside. I squeeze a head gently, testing for firmness. Soft? I tear apart the outer leaves and poke into the core. Pale green ooze soaks my fingers. I check the rest. Sodden! I have disgusting slime infection throughout the bed.

My head reels. Can I salvage **any** lettuce harvest? I painstakingly examine every plant in each bed. I must harvest very selectively. Even a little touch of slime means that even the good leaves will taste bitter.

Strange. Normally lettuces are so trouble-free to raise in our cool Alaskan climate. Yet I have discovered entire lettuce beds that are diseased and unsuitable to sell. I am usually so proud of my vast harvests of lettuce varieties. I cannot imagine **not** growing these colorful salad greens for my customers.

What brought on this outburst? And what can I do about this slime and tip burn?

I need the most expert information available — so why not tune in? I'm feeling more experienced at this process. Now then, do I call on the Lettuce Deva? Or the Slime Deva? Or the Deva of Soil? Oh, well! I request a whole council of Devas: soil, lettuces, and the microbes causing these diseases.

Ellen: Welcome, dear consulting council! I am discouraged about all this slime and tip burn damage. I guess you'd say my kids are spoiled rotten. Why is infection so rampant here this summer?

Lettuce Deva Council: *June was just too hot and sunny for lettuces. Your recent hot spell contributed to the severity of the diseases. It hit at a critical time in the life cycle of the developing lettuce varieties.*

Ellen: I quietly note to myself that I received the answer I was looking for. I did not know if I would hear from a sorrowful lettuce, a victorious bacterium, or the perspective of soil minerals. Whew! I ask, "What can I do in the future when we experience this kind of weather?"

Devas: *Next year, try planting the lettuces in partial shade, or perhaps cover with a shade cloth.*

Ellen: What can be rescued or salvaged now?

Devas: *For the infected lettuce that is mature now, it's too far gone for rescue or rehabilitation. Salvage the outside leaves for your household to eat, if you can.*

Ellen: As I clean out the diseased beds, where do I put the slimed lettuces? I don't want to spread infection. Is it safe to compost them?

Devas: *Cleanup is essential. That helps to decrease re-infection. Compost-*

ing is slightly more effective at reducing slime disease than rototilling. The best prevention tactic would be to remove all slimed lettuce from the garden. Gather up all remnants that you can and discard them.

Ellen: "Discard" means take garbage bags of them to the dump? (I try to avoid generating waste that has to go to the landfill.)

Devas: *Yes. The dump is a good place to dispose of your infected lettuces.*

Ellen: What else about cleanup?

Devas: *Do an energy cleansing process.*

Ellen: You mean adapt Machaelle Small Wright's procedure for this situation? Exactly how?

Devas: *Yes. Again, imagine a filter cloth, and place it under the lettuce beds, just under the roots. Ask that as you lift the cloth, that you catch all the results and effects of the slime in your filter. Then ask the Nature Spirits to clean and polish. Ask them to clean up and set everything straight after the slime is removed.*

Ellen: Then will it be safe to grow lettuces in those same areas again?

Devas: *No. Do not plant or transplant new lettuce seedlings into the infected areas. When they are young, the plants are weaker and are more vulnerable to slime.*

Ellen: Okay. Does excessive dampness trigger slime growth, too?

Devas: *Yes. As your next crops of lettuces mature and leaf out, irrigate from a sprinkler that delivers water above the plants. Your soaker hoses underneath the plants leave more moisture trapped at ground level.*

Ellen: Thanks so much! I am relieved to hear your specific instructions. As a market gardener, I **do** want to continue growing salad-makings for my customers each year.

I dig and haul, change my watering system, do the cleansing, and invite the Nature Spirits to my cleanup party. When July is finally over, I rejoice. And sure enough, later lettuce plantings in new beds do much better.

The following two summers are cooler, and my lettuce crops give me healthy yield. Whew! I find slime only in the red Romaine, so I quit growing that variety.

Then comes 1995. I irrigate my way through an unusually scorching hot and dry June. Slime strikes again in early July. What was I told to do about this? I forget. I have to look back in my trusty spiral notebook.

I am grateful to review explicit written directions. A tune-in would have required me to stop, adjust my state of mind, quiet myself, formulate questions, and write down impressions. Now I can go right to work with those drastic but preventive measures. The results? That next summer, I enjoy healthy lettuce crops. Slime infection does not spread and take over. Hurrah! I can still revel in parenting my colorful lettuce selections and harvest abundantly. The success continues forward into several summers.

Once again, the Deva's recommendations for disease management prove reliable. You know, I am finally trusting these Devas and Nature Spirits.

Note: Please see Appendix 3 for a review of the Energy

Cleansing Process; the above is an adaptation.

Rain Dance

WE ARE STUCK in **drought**! We've had no rain from mid-May and now it is mid-July. Grass, trees, and garden greens are so thirsty. Dry wind adds its insult to glaring high afternoon sun. These are the weeks that my baby vegetables need rain the very most. I irrigate and irrigate. The sprinkler delivers water, but it's just not the same as rain.

Finally, today, a tiny drizzle begins to fall. Jan Pohl is visiting again, and we all watch from inside, rejoicing... for a minute. The rain ceases altogether, and the sky clears again. The moisture is not enough to penetrate more than an eighth inch (3 mm) into the soil. This little bit of dampness will never reach the roots of anything.

Augh! What now? Three of us tune in to the Overlighting Angel of the Garden and ask if there is anything we can do. We hope to learn how to bring more rain clouds.

Garden Angel: *Go outside and dance! Dance in the rain.*

Huh? This sounds crazy! Did we hear that answer correctly? That rain was only a tiny sprinkle. We ask for elaboration.

Garden Angel: *Yes, that's right. Thank the rain. Dance and dance for joy. Your dancing will amplify the benefit of the rain. Dance it down into the soil. Expand its depth and blessing.*

The Garden Angel signs off with another unexpected comment: *If Fay wants to, she can stay in and take a little nap. That is just as important as dance in the great scheme of things.*

Jan, being her usual playful self, jumps up and says, "Let's go!" She bounds out the door and onto the front lawn. I hesitantly follow her.

What are we doing? What do we do? Are any neighbors watching? Are they seriously questioning our sanity? I know we asked for guidance, but now I am doubting and discounting.

Whoosh, there goes Jan, merrily skipping around the yard. Oh, well! We circle and cheer. We whoop, stomp, and whirl. We dance the rain into the Earth. We must be. Who are we to know any better than Mother Nature? And who are we to know the real benefits of dance amidst the perception of drought?

Whom To Call Upon?

WE ARE getting experienced in the tune-in process, but now we are very curious. When we have a specific question, and want to tune in for the answer, just whom do we invoke? The topics vary. Are we to seek a specialist for the topic? How would we know which one, exactly? Might this exclude other beings with helpful input? Or do we invite a more general Deva?

A weed question, for example, might be referenced to that plant's spirit, but the weed is intertwined with soil, insects, neighboring plant community, and larger ecosystem. Whom should we invoke? Likewise, should a question about soil balancing include calling in the Deva of atmosphere, because of the cosmic influences on soil? How do we address all the members of the microscopic soil food web? Wouldn't that consist of Nature Spirits as well as Devas of fungi, bacteria, protozoa and nematodes? So whom ought we to call upon?

Janice Schofield and I tune in to ask about this when I visit her in Homer, Alaska. We decided to simply put out the question to Spirit in general. Then we quieted ourselves to receive from whomever answered. These are the responses, and they feel like excellent guidance to use all the time.

When you send a question, it sends out a signal, like a gong. This signal travels and permeates the realms. We recommend you proceed like this.

1. *Ask your question.*
2. *Give thanks for the answer.*
3. *Receive the information*

You are surrounded by beings who love you. Specialists will answer from their area of expertise. You need not grope and guess for which one to ask.

If you do designate a Being, then that one Being is a spokesperson for the others who have the most information on your topic.

Slugs –
Invasion Strikes

"OH, ELLEN, everything you've heard is true. They are terrible," exclaims Kate Nilsson, my Anchorage gardening friend. She usually took everything in her stride, but today she is wringing her hands with exasperation.

"Each day, I'm picking 40-70 slugs off each head of lettuce. Crews of chewing slugs have strip-mined my nearly maturing cabbage to sickly skeletons. It only took them two days!

"Those slugs have invaded everywhere — even in my herbs, carrot tops, flowers, and the prickly leaves of radishes! I've never seen that before. Oh, my precious tomatoes in pots in the deck! When I saw what slugs do to tomatoes, it made me lose my appetite. I give up on them. You can forget trying to grow squash and beans, too.

"Once slugs get started, they are almost impossible to get rid of. I'm thinking of abandoning my garden in Anchorage. I can't keep up with hand-picking 250 slugs per night in the garden. If you can, I advise you to avoid slugs!"

"Gosh," I brood, "I just moved to Palmer. I haven't heard any reports of slugs in the Matanuska Valley, where we just bought land to create a huge market garden."

"Keep it that way!" Kate replied. "I'm envious." Kate is a trained Permaculture School graduate, accustomed to pest challenges in several climates. Gardening to her is an essential ingredient of living.

Other Anchorage gardeners quickly echo Kate's horror stories. The exploding population of slugs is on the march all over the city. They are like Viking invaders —ransacking and advancing at an alarming rate. These tales of destruction make me a believer. I do not want to deal with slugs! My new garden is my hope for a new entrepreneurship. I vow resistance!

So what are these slugs like? How do I keep them out?

I study the enemy. I learn that this formidable creature, so capable of despoiling acts, actually has a vulnerably soft body. A slug is but a snail without a shell. It keeps itself coated with slime. A slug has no legs, and a head protrudes eyeballs on stems. The Anchorage variety has a beige or brown body. Full-grown, it measures only one and half inches (3.75cm) long. This is intellectually interesting but ICK!.

How do I keep out a pest that moves fast on one foot, rasps leaves to skeletons, and breeds faster than rabbits?

Oh, oh. I learn too late.

It isn't until several months later that I see my horticultural mentor, Jean Bochenek. Jean tells me that, for all the years she operated a greenhouse in Anchorage, she never heard of slugs. Not in Anchorage. Today's species are a recent import. Nurseries and landscapers have unwittingly shipped them to Alaska from the west coast states in potted plants, shrubs, and trees. Every importation of plant materials from outside Alaska runs the risk of importing slugs. Slugs or slug eggs in the soil can hitch-hike in with any shipment of shrubs, berry bushes, trees, and perennials. Since slugs lay clusters of 7-15 eggs, their population can mushroom exponentially in one season.

Jean warns me to be careful that I don't bring slugs out to the Valley in transplants, firewood, or anything!

Oh, oh!

Jean teaches me this a year and a half too late. I had already proudly moved my Anchorage compost heap out here. I blithely brought old Anchorage lumber to this yard. I innocently transplanted a little cherry tree from my old place. I encourage some people from Eagle River (right next to Anchorage) to drop off bags and bags of grass clippings for compost and mulch.

Good heavens, I have personally aided in colonizing slug starter kits in the greater Palmer area. Wow! I wonder how many other escapees from Anchorage have seeded slugs in this rapidly-suburbanizing area we call the Matanuska-Sustina Valley?

I begin looking around nervously.

I spy two slugs in the long grass bordering the garden. Augh! No! A few weeks later, I find two more on the edge of the well pit door. I do not want to talk with them. I just want them to go away. Even if I can eliminate them on our property, the slugs can spread to a neighbor's yard, and lay more and more eggs. Help! I don't want a population explosion!

Bam, bam! I smash them with my shovel. How many more slugs have taken root around here?

The following spring as I plant the garden, I try to ignore and deny the possibility of silent but stealthy growth of slug armies. Eventually, I spot another individual. Aha — the enemy! I raise my weapon. My churning panic drives me to lash out with a vengeance. Stamp out every one, now! Before slugs devour my livelihood!

I freeze in mid-swing. I have to admit it. I feel uncomfortable with my escalating fears and readiness for war. I am turning into an angry lynch mob of one. This is exactly what I want to avoid. Gardening should be more fun than this. Had not Findhorn demonstrated another way? I put down my weapon, trembling.

I have to face up to this. I resolve to try conversation first. Quivering in my boots, I ask Fay for assistance in tuning in. It goes like this.

Fay & Ellen: Deva of slugs of the specie I've met here on the property, may we please be in contact with your collective consciousness?

Ellen: I hope we are consciously connected. I can't tell, possibly because of my aversion and resistance. I can't tell because I am scared of you. That is, I've been scared to find you here. I've been scared to talk with you. I have been wishing you could all just disappear. I have feared that my market garden and my way of making a living will be ruined like the gardens in Anchorage. I have a knot in my tummy about having to quit farming.

But I affirm that this garden is a place of balance. I would like to ask you to join in the balancing act. If you exist here, I'd like you to keep your numbers low so we do not have an over-population of slugs.

Are we in contact, and would you consider such an arrangement?

Slug deva: (This is one of the rare times in which I actually heard words of communication in my head, and the words blasted me with an emphatic punch.)

Population? POPULATION! It's the humans who have a population explosion! We try *to stay in balance, and we* want *to stay in balance. But our species reflects the energies of the humans. There are too many people, and they live too close together. We cannot help it. We pick up their chaotic thinking, stress, and frenzy. The result is that we multiply faster than we want to. We don't like it either. But what can we do, trying to live within an environment that is so energetically charged?*

If people would keep their population in control, we could do the same!

Humans around here should learn the nature of balance, instead of telling us to mind some balance of nature!

Fay & Ellen: Whew! It's one thing for us humans to hold the opinion that we have too many people on the planet, and that there are adverse effects of our population explosion. It's quite another to hear an angel confirm that! We did not know that human over-breeding fuels your birth rates as well!

If humans should ever get their reproductive rates under control, what would happen to your slug population growth rates?

Slug Deva: *Our species would be affected directly, and we would experience corresponding adjustments in our population levels.*

Ellen: Sadly, it is not likely that humans will do this voluntarily any time soon. Is there a way that we can work out a cooperative bargain with you here at Good Earth Gardens? Can you just disappear?

Slug Deva: *Whew! That is asking a lot. No, we cannot just disappear. When you transport us to a new location that is where we take up residence. We did not ask to be here, but it has become our home. You brought us here. We are established here. As the Deva, I produce the life form of slugs. That is my job. That is a Deva's commitment. Asking me to hold back is like trying to stop a waterfall.*

Still, you are asking for cooperation, and that too is our nature. Let us think about this. Contact us tomorrow.

Fay and I disconnect and review the emotional blast, and the news that the slug forms cannot just disappear. I am relieved to take a break until tomorrow.

Slugs –
Next Day, the Bargain

Fay & Ellen: We're back! Deva of our slugs, may we please be in conscious connection with you?

We thank you so much for being willing to talk with us, help us, and consider ways to accomplish population management. We acknowledge that this is contrary to your Devic nature. It contradicts your instincts and basic nature to survive and multiply. It is people who accelerate your rate of multiplication. It sounds like we humans need to accept our responsibility. Our own population growth and chaotic behaviors cause you imbalance, as do our habits of directly transporting you slugs to new areas.

We are excited to work with you. What ideas have you come up with?

Slug Deva: (Fay receives the following extensive communication by hearing a voice in her head. It comes through with clarity. I get very little — perhaps some vague notion here and there. Fay repeats aloud what she hears from the Deva. I finally relax into this pattern and quit straining to get slug communication. I sit back and concentrate on the questions I want to ask, then I listen to Fay's voice transmit the answers.)

Yes, holding back is contradictory to my purpose of producing this life form, i.e. this species of slugs.

You have some areas that are very moist and appealing to us slugs. One is your "wild area," as you call it. This edge of mature trees and the long grass under them is a place that stays wet longer than the lawn. Another area is alongside the house. The roof drips on the soil here, and ornamentals around the foundation keep it shaded. We love moisture! Another is your compost area and garden. Compost is inviting. Your vegetables are inviting. Items like ash are less inviting. We don't like ash. Spread ash where you do not want us.

Ellen: Well, you said you were established here. What would you like as your area?

Slugs: (Sounding very excited and more animated.) *What would we like?! Oh, thank you for asking!!! (With a jubilant tone) We would like to claim the following areas:*

1. *The front of the house. We'd like blanket permission to use the damp corridor, the north edge along the house, from the elderberry bush to the porch.*

2. *A portion of the woods that you call the wild area, by the side plot. We would like a section of this wild area, bordered by the fallen tree, the wire fence, the trail to the dog coop, and the side garden plot. Could this be the one place that slugs can be? We would like this spot as a sanctuary.*

3. *The old compost heap by the side plot that you imported. May we have part of that in our area, with no ash on it? Make a special compost pile for us.*

Ellen: You are very clear about what you would like. I think I can picture the general areas. Those locations are very reasonable requests, and they are not large. Probably your forms are living in there, anyway.

Yes, your proposal sounds very fair to me. We'll call these designated or permitted areas. Yes, you can have the area you suggested as your sanctuary. I'll do some rearranging there, and move the pile more in the center of your sanctuary for you. Then I'll dedicate it as "The Slug Sanctuary".

Will your forms know the boundaries? Can they recognize them when they crawl up to them?

Slugs: *We'll be somewhat aware, but it would be so much better if you could help us by marking the boundaries.*

Ellen: How do I mark them to help you stay within bounds?

Slugs: *Sprinkle a heavy strip or band of wood ash along the borders. Make the application about 4-6" (9-13 cm) wide.*

Fay: Let's see if I can draw a picture. I think I see what the deva is describing. (She works up a sketch.) Does this represent the specific boundaries you are proposing?

Slugs: *That's a very good drawing. Yes, we concur.*

Ellen: You'll need a path to go back and forth from the sanctuary to the front of the house, won't you?

Slugs: *Oh, yes, that would be wonderful!*

Ellen: Okay. You want bands of ash on the ground to outline your boundaries. Then you want a "de-militarized zone" where you are allowed to be. Now I'm trying to visualize that pile you mentioned. You want a relocated compost heap? Please say more.

Slugs: *Make it large, rather large.*

Ellen: I don't get it.

Slugs: *Mound it up. Put it in the middle of our sanctuary. Make it rather large. Make it by moving the old, existing pile. Give us about half of its material. Wet it down for us.*

Ellen: What is it for?

Slugs: *This would be a splendid playground for us.*

Ellen: A playground? My goodness, you sound so formal and serious. It did not occur to me that you'd like a place to play.

Slugs: *Oh, yes!*

Fay: I'm getting a picture of a mountain… that's how the new pile would look to a slug. I see little comical slugs with knapsacks, climbing to the top. The first group reach the peak and plant a flag on a pole!

Ellen: Well, we are learning more about you. Thanks for this session, Deva of Slugs. I'll get to work with the ashes from the wood stove. I'll sprinkle boundaries and set up your playground. We'll close for now, and reconnect later as I develop more questions.

Slugs – A Name and a Magic Prescription

A FEW DAYS later, Fay delivers this surprise announcement, "Ellie, I'm getting a repeating message in my head. The Slug Deva would like you to call him."

Oh? Okay!

Fay & Ellen: Deva of the Species of Slugs in our yard, we ask to be back in conscious connection with you. (We waited a few seconds until we felt connected, and then proceed.) What would you like us to know?

Fay: (Again, Fay hears the Deva's communication in her head, and relays it aloud to me.) Ellie, this is what this Deva is telling me. When the slugs want to get your attention, they'd like to devise a signal. They are proposing a method. The Slug Deva says that it will first try contacting my mind. If that doesn't work, a slug will get your attention by sitting on the first step of the front landing. Check those steps in your coming and goings. But any of us can initiate contact at any time we feel the desire.

Ellen: Great! While we are on the line, I have more questions, Slug Deva. First, do you have a name you'd like to be called, besides "Deva of Slugs"?

Slug Deva: (Again, Fay is able to hear Devic transmissions in sentences and dictate them aloud to me. I get nothing directly.) *Yes, you can call me "Bob, the Slug Deva. Actually, "Robert" would be more exact.*

Fay: He sounds just like our scientific friend, Bob Jones. He chooses his words precisely and objectively.

Ellen: Very well, we'll call you "Robert"! By the way, I've constructed your mountain. Is that what you had in mind?

Robert: *Excellent.*

Ellen: You want it moist?

Robert: *Keep it wet for the next while. Cover it with black plastic, too.*

Ellen: I've harvested ash from the wood stove, screened it, and spread the ash along those borders. We now have a slug fence — of ash. Do you want anything else?

Robert: *Keep your driveway swept clean of leaves and dirt, especially by the door and front landing. The cement is harsh on slug flesh, so it makes a good fence, too.*

Ellen: Okay. By the way, do you have any natural predators?

Robert: *Mice find and eat some of our eggs. Occasionally, a bird eats an adult slug. You don't have toads in this bioregion.*

Ellen: What are the priority areas for additional ash?

Robert: *Each of your 3 compost piles needs a ring of protection. Make a wide ash border around them, just like the borders for the zones you delineated. Do the same for the garden plots. Outline each plot with a heavy band of ash. Keep maintaining these strips.*

Fay: I rarely get pictures during these communications, but this time I see an aerial view of our three major plots. I see red around the edges of each, where the ash should go.

Robert: *From now on, spread ash on top of each of your garden plots, too. Do it after rototilling. This year, since it is fall and your matured crops are in the way, spread the ash on the paths between the vegetable rows.*

Ellen: On the footpaths? Doesn't the ash need to be under the vegetables to effectively deter slugs? It looks impossible for me to try to reach under each full-grown cabbage, all the potato vines, the zucchini, and broccoli.

Robert: *Ash can be expanded. After you put it on the paths, ask the nature spirits to spread it into the beds.*

Ellen: How? And will the ash turn the soil pH too alkaline for optimal vegetable growth?

Robert: *Invite the Nature Spirits, me, the Deva of Ash, and the Deva of Soil to join you. State your goal and request. Ask the Nature Spirits to spread the ash onto the soil in the beds. Ask that they shift an appropriate amount to repel slugs but not to adversely raise the pH of the soil. Lend your energy for this task.*

Ellen: Wow, this is great! Thank you for cooking up a special procedure just for my situation, Robert!

I march out and give this a try. I can actually feel a bustling and a shifting of matter. The Nature Spirits entertain me with humorous imagery as they work. I laugh out loud. This is fun!

Slugs – Is Anyone Else Talking to You?

IT FEELS GOOD to be communicating with the slugs after my months of nagging fear. I wonder: are we pioneering? Are other people communicating with them, too? Perhaps the slugs have developed a standard list of recommendations.

So I ask, "Robert, are there other people talking to you?"

Robert answers, *Not with words I like to hear.*

His tone of voice is light-hearted, but I get the point. Most talk directed at slugs is the cursing kind! Robert's tone, and the inner smile I feel, tells me he harbors no ill-will in return.

Slugs –
Boundaries and Repellants

"HELLO AGAIN, Robert the Slug Deva! Thank you for being here. We have questions for you," I explain, opening another consultation with our unseen friend.

"I found an individual slug who was out of bounds. He was in the back lawn, heading for the compost complex. This adult was way beyond the sanctuary. What should I do about these violators?

Robert: (Again, Fay relays the message). *There are not supposed to be any slugs in the back yard. Not every slug goes along with the group consciousness. There are rebels. As the Deva, I cannot command and guarantee control of each individual. These rebels are ones that I don't want in the back yard. When you find them, get rid of them.*

Fay: Do you mean carry them back to the permitted area?

Robert: *Ah, tender-hearted Fay. No, I mean exterminate the rebels. I do not want any slugs in the back yard. Please do so for our mutual help, per our agreement. Thank them for being, and then squash them or whatever. A quick death is always appreciated.*

Ellen: This is very generous of you to recommend killing, since as a Deva you promote the life of your form, which in your case is slugs. I appreciate your adaptation for our bargain. Thank you for this. Now then, do I need to conduct a thorough hunt for rebels?

Robert: *You are welcome. Death is not a bad thing, and your patrolling helps our mutual agreement. And no, a hunt is not necessary. Just take care of the trespassers as you see them.*

Ellen: What about my compost piles? I understand that compost is a luscious attraction to slugs. I read that slugs have an excellent sense of smell to locate compost in all its stages of breakdown. I want to keep them out. Do I also apply ash to these piles as a deterrent?

Robert: *Keep maintaining borders of ash around your piles, as we'd talked about. If slugs and eggs get a foothold in compost piles, slugs will be spread everywhere as you spread finished compost on the garden plots.*

So, yes, add ash to the piles themselves. You've been instructed by the Deva of Soil about adding wood ash to compost piles. This is a second reason to incorporate ash-it's slug protection.

Ellen: What do I ask for?

Robert: *For this, ask for assistance from me as well as the Nature Spirits and Deva of Soil. Request that this team please mix enough ash into the compost pile to prevent slugs, without upsetting the soil's pH balance for optimal vegetable growth.*

Ellen: Robert, thank you for this exciting counsel! You've given us more magic tools.

Slugs –
A Set-Up

"ROBERT, I've been wondering about something. Every time we tune in to you, Fay hears you clearly in her head. She hears you speaking in words, sentences, and paragraphs. Your communication is always formal and factual. Your transmissions are logical and sequential. Meanwhile, I get no pictures, words, or impressions... nothing. Does this mean that Fay is a skilled channel of your spirit?

Robert: (Emphatically) *I am NOT being channeled! I am talking directly to you!*

Ellen: Whew! I stand corrected. But I don't hear your communication. Why? Is my mind deficient?

Robert: *Actually, this has nothing to do with you, Ellie. This is about Fay. It's a gift to help her to trust this tune-in process. We cooked this up for Fay.*

Ellen: You did? Why?

Robert: *She is still recovering from her Christian fundamentalist upbringing. I am helping her be at ease with your attunement process.*

Ellen: Fay, do you understand what Robert is saying?

Fay: Oh, absolutely yes, I know what he's getting at. Ellie, you think that quieting your mind and opening to spiritual messages is a natural thing. If you receive tunes, thoughts, and pictures, you accept them as forms of communication. In my years of church training, I was taught that such opening is an invitation to the devil.

Ellen: The devil? I am shocked. Why?

Fay: My religion emphatically taught me that real prayer is not a process of seeking direct answers. Rather, prayer means asking God to give you something, or imploring God to do something. I was indoctrinated for years with church instruction that God speaks only through the Bible. One should seek answers from the Bible or church sermons, period.

Ellen: What is the harm in seeking heavenly guidance?

Fay: Looking for guidance from within your Self would get you into spiritual trouble. Looking to nature for guidance would be deliberately stepping into deeper trouble. Praying to trees and animals might connect you with a spirit, but it would not be God's spirit. It would be a false god, an evil force. It might seem fine at the time, but it will lead to your eventual downfall. Nature, you see, is Satan's realm. I have had these ideas drilled into me for years. From the pulpit, Sunday School, and Bible Study groups, I have been strongly admonished to limit my trust to God and words in the Bible.

Ellen: This sounds like the joke:

> *"When people speak to God, it's called prayer.*
> *When God speaks to people, it's called schizophrenia."*
> *-Lily Tomlin*

Fay: Yes, that is exactly what the fundamentalists have drilled into my head.

Ellen: So Robert, what strategy have you been using?

Robert: *When Fay tunes in to me, the Deva of Slugs, I speak to Fay in words. I avoid pictures so I won't scare her. When I sound as carefully worded and non-threatening as your scientist friend Bob Jones, I help her accept and trust this communication with angelic realms.*

Fay and I have a good laugh. This is a Devic joke. There has been a good reason why I never receive any Devic conversation from the slugs. This is staged for Fay! Robert sounds just like our learned friend who helps us in the garden. Robert (Bob) Jones is a retired scientist for the U.S. Fish and Wildlife Service who is famous for his otter and waterfowl studies in the Aleutian Islands.

Ellen: I'm still amazed at the doctrine. Is this really what your church background taught you Fay? You've told me that you are a recovering fundamentalist, but now I am beginning to understand.

Fay: Yes, it's true. And yes, when I recite to you what I hear from the Slug Deva, I feel like I am sitting at the table, conversing with Bob Jones. I hear his precise, scientific, objective style. It is very non-threatening. So, thanks, Deva Robert! You are helping me re-condition! By the way, what are you really like?

Robert: (With the feeling of a smile and casual tone.) *Oh, I'm probably a little more light-hearted than your dear human friend.*

Slugs –
Ash Prevention Regimen

I AM dashing down the basement stairs when I see it. Even in my harvest season rush, I notice something in the casement window. There, gracefully working its way through a small hole in the metal screen is a slug!

What are the odds that a slug would choose a path that rasps its soft flesh on dry metal mesh... **and** find the only one-inch (2.5cm) hole in all of the window screens?

Ha! The odds are extremely low, I realize. This must be Robert and his humorous antics to get my attention. What a creative variation on the "appear on the front step" signal!

Fay and I tune in that evening.

Ellen: You rang, Robert? I got your message! You make me grin. How is it that I can love you so much, and still be repulsed at your slimy form? What's up?

Robert: (With urgency) *Can you get more ash?*

Ellen: Yes, from the scout camp and neighbors. Why?

Robert: *The ash washes away when you irrigate or it rains. This leaches out the strength of the ash fences. You'll need a lot more to replenish all your borders around composting areas, garden plots, and the sanctuary, especially in long grass.*

Ellen: I'll work on getting more ash today. What else can I do to retard slug damage and population build-up?

Robert: *Keep re-coating borders with ash after rain and irrigating. Or use diatomaceous earth instead of ash, but it will still need occasional replacing. Better still, mix diatomaceous earth with alum (a chemical salt).*

Remember that in the rainy season, no barrier will be perfect. When the material is wet, our forms (slugs) can crawl right over it. Rain makes us mobile.

It's been raining steadily, and we can hardly concentrate on this tune-in. We are on the march to explore new worlds! Conditions are perfect. Off we go!

Fay & Ellen: Okay, dear Robert, and thank you! Over and out!

Recipe for Alum and Diatomaceous Earth (DE)

Mix 4 parts diatomaceous earth (DE) with one part alum (a chemical salt). Don't use DE for swimming pool systems; it is less sharp. Spread this mixture the same way you apply ash borders. Just be sure to wear goggles and a dust mask when you handle it, so the diatomaceous earth dust does not tear up your eyes or lungs. Please see Appendix 1B for explanation of DE.

Slugs –
Beer and Scanning

Ellen: "Robert, all the experts say use beer traps. My trap line of brew catches nothing. What do you advise?"

Robert: *"When you put out yogurt containers with some beer in the bottom, recess the traps. Put the top lip of the container at surface level. You could even put the sunken containers in a series with a board loosely over the trap line.*

Ellie, do you intend to use this September's leaves and grass clippings from your lawn in your composting or mulching operations?"

Ellen: "Yes. It's hard for me to pass up all that organic matter under my nose".

Robert: *"Don't do it. I cannot guarantee that the material will be slug-less. Let the clippings decompose where they should — right back into the lawn."*

Come early spring, resist collecting the leaves alongside your house. Do inspection and prevention instead. Make spring cleanup the time when you rake and burn all those leaves. You'll be destroying eggs and over-wintering adults from this moist perimeter."

Ellen: "Okay, Robert, you are the authority here. What else for spring clean up?"

Robert: *"Don't stop with raking. Overturn rocks, boards, leaf piles, plastic mulch, and any other piles of stuff. These are likely to harbor our slug forms and eggs. Use a weed burner or spray to kill eggs."*

Ellen: "What kind of spray?"

Robert: *"Choose either a bleach or ammonia solution. And Ellie, if you really must scavenge lumber and firewood at the Borough dump, check with me first!"*

Ellen: "How? What do I ask for?"

Robert: "*Wait until you are physically there, as you are examining a load of wood. Ask me if there are slugs present on the item. You cannot see them, but I can. If there is only one slug or a single egg in the lumber, it is too much. Reject it, or scrub it thoroughly with a dry, stiff-bristled floor brush. Especially scour the ends of boards. Collect all scrubbings and take them to the dump in a tightly sealed garbage bag.*

Do not accept or bring in ANY transplants, grass clippings, firewood, barn waste, leaves, or other organic matter without checking with me. One imported slug or egg can quickly mushroom into many, who multiply quickly into more than you or I can control."

Fay & Ellen: Wow, thank you Robert, for your thorough counsel. We especially appreciate your detail about destroying eggs, bagging, etc. Again, we are grateful that you honor our bargain by altering your Devic blueprint and advising slug population management.

Robert: *Again you are welcome.*

I admit that reform is difficult for this hard-core scavenger! But given the hope of controlling slug numbers, I train myself to remember the routine. If I find tempting lumber at the dump, I resist loading it. I wait, find Fay and take her back with me. We tune in and ask Robert if he can see any slugs present. Robert answers with quips like *"Slug Free"* to the tune of *"Born Free."* Or he'll say, *"Oh, no! Do not take that."* One time we asked Robert if there were carpenter ants present, since we did not want to import them, either. Robert replied, *"My job is slugs."* We chuckled.

People generously offer me loads of manure and bedding waste, yard trimmings, etc. I never dare give a yes or no until I have Robert scan it.

Long distance scanning is another matter, we learned. I saw a bulletin offering free tons of poultry manure at the Totem Egg Farm near Wasilla. I am not familiar with the location. I ask Robert to scope the slug status for me before driving over there. I am surprised — Robert does not know.

He explains, *We devas, we are not necessarily all-knowing. We have limits to knowledge. If you have never been there, I cannot look through your eyes and check for slugs.*

In contrast, when Janice Schofield visits in Palmer, she asks Robert for advice on slug management for her place in Homer. Homer is a 6-hour drive away. Even though Jan's slugs are a slightly different species and thus a slightly different Deva, Robert can do a long distance assessment this time. He can see Jan's land through her as she stands in Palmer. He specifically suggests that she cut up all the downed wood on the property to eliminate slug habitat. He recommends that she continue her attitude of respect and willingness to tune in.

Robert informs Jan that she is not having as severe an impact from slugs as her neighbor because she is not slaughtering them with toilet bowl cleaner.

Recipe for Slug Egg Spray

Mix 1 cup bleach to 4 cups water, or 1cup ammonia plus 4 cups water. **Never combine bleach and ammonia.** The resulting fumes are lethal. Choose one or the other. Ammonia serves as a nitrogen fertilizer on the soil, whereas chlorine bleach products kill soil food web microbes. Wear a dust mask and goggles. The spray will kill eggs. This strength is enough to kill slug babies, too, if they have hatched.

Slugs –
Sex and Play

DO YOU REMEMBER Robert's unique message system? He told me to check the front steps regularly as I traverse from house to garden and back. If I spot a slug on the steps, this means, "Get in touch with me!"

One morning I step outside, look down, and spot not one but two slugs on the lowest front step. Robert must **really** want me to attune to him. I look closer. These two are coupled. They are luxuriously and sensually mating. There is no hurry as they intertwine.

Wow, what a privilege to see this! I wonder how many other humans have experienced this. To the biologist in me, this is a delightful gift. The process is fascinating! One slug extends a cone-like apparatus from its side. This cone fits into a tiny round opening in the partner slug's side. Does this mean that there are male and female slugs? How do slug reproductive systems compare to earthworms? Where do eggs form and how are they laid? When I tune in to thank Robert for such an honorary show, he smiles and remarks, "I thought you'd like that."

Another day, I see a slug on the pavement, but not alone. Little springtails (*Collembola sp.*) the size of pencil dots are surrounding the slug, hopping around. A few springtails are landing on the slug's body. We asked Robert what that feels like to the slug. Robert describes the experience through Fay's body. "Oooh!" she chuckles. "It's a sensation of playing, of delight, of ecstasy! Both species are enjoying the interaction immensely!"

Gosh, Robert, I had no idea that mighty outbursts of joy are happening all over the ground I walk!

Slugs – A Slug Speaks Hawk Language

THAT HAWK is diving right at me! Where did he come from!? And again! Right over my head! What the heck is this all about?

I am still curious as I cast off my pack after my hike on Old Baldy Mountain today. That hawk swooped within 10 feet (3m.) of me. It circled in the sky and dived towards me three more times, hovering a bit each time. This hawk did not pounce or scream, but he was deliberately weaving close to me. Startling... and strange! This is sub-alpine country. It's not the place I'd expect a hawk to nest, and nesting season is over. This bird of prey was not acting protectively — I felt like he was inspecting me. I tried attuning to the hawk by myself, but I could not discern a message.

"Fay," I muse as I unlace my hiking boots, "do you think Robert can tell us what was going on? Let's set up a three-way hook up and see if it works!"

"Do you mean, ask the slug consciousness to look into your episode to see if the hawk was sending a message? This should be interesting," Fay reflects, intrigued.

"Yes." We jump in.

Robert, may we please be in contact with you? Would you like to try being an inter-species interpreter for us?

Robert pipes up enthusiastically, *This will be fun to try!*

Fay and I visualize a three-way link-up and I focus on my hawk drama. Like a Hollywood film, audio-visuals begin rolling in our human minds. I see a swirling of blue and then an owl's face.

Robert understands and elaborates. *Ellie, your aura and the hawk's aura intermingle and vastly expand each other's size.*

I think about my fleeting picture of an owl — is this a clue that the bird that showed itself to me is a species called a hawk owl (*Surnia ulula*)?

Fay hears the hawk say, *I am the eyes of the mountain. I constantly track the action here, and let the others know.*

Next I feel/see this hawk dancing in the sky. I hear a succession of tunes in my head, starting with, "We know we belong to land, and the land we belong to is grand!" Ha! It's the show tune from the musical production, *Oklahoma*!

More audio communications play inside my head. I smile to hear the rousing, celebrative waltz theme from the musical *Carousel*. This fades as victorious strains of Handel's *Messiah* burst forth. "Blessing and honor and power and glory to be unto Him, be unto Him..."

Now I see an infant taking baby steps. "I'm baffled, Robert! What does this mean?" Robert explains. *This symbolizes your first attempts to work with the Devas and Nature Spirits.*

My inner picture-show changes scenes again. I am shown a hawk's eye view of Good Earth Gardens. I see a pathway cleared... then the aura of the property gets cleaned. Fay catches the meaning. The land begins to radiate a white light as we invite spiritual help, welcome all life forms, and release negativity. The land shines with the glory of God. When Fay explains this, I see a new picture in my mind. It's a baby enjoying a sudsy hair wash. "What's this, Robert?" *This symbolizes the caring and cleansing you do in the garden, Ellie and Fay.*

My eyes moisten. I am flabbergasted. This is the view on an energetic level? Our actions affect the land this way? Here at Good Earth Gardens? Now that is truly environmental impact! I had no idea.

We eventually collect ourselves and close. "Thank you so much, Robert, for serving as interpreter and endearing us even further."

Months later, I remember Robert's marvelous help. I ask Fay to assist me for another link-up. We attune and I ask, "Can you interpret again, Robert? I would love your help. I'm stumped by a vague message from another Deva. Can you amplify for me?

Robert: *I'm looking into the matter, and I have to decline. I want to help. I like to be of help. In this situation, however, it is best for you to keep trying directly. It will better for you to see what you can get for yourself.*

Ellen: Oh, shucks. I haven't gotten very far. I'm not sure that I can.

I try putting clues together like a detective. Nothing. I finally resort to just letting the non-sensical images float in my head for several days. I vow to stay open and honest. Slowly, this dream-like collage makes sense. It is symbolic, and showing me a parallel a pattern in my behavior. Aha!

Robert is right again! Persistence pays!

Slugs –
What to Reveal, Robert?

ROBERT is absolutely right. Once humans bring slugs into an area, slug populations fan out like forest fires.

Gardeners are reporting mass slug invasions throughout the entire Kenai Peninsula and the Matanuska-Susitna Valley. One rainy afternoon in Homer, I can hardly walk on the sidewalk without stepping on a slug, so I count them. I tally an average of 9-13 slugs per square yard (square metre) of concrete. That's fast procreation and migration. It's only been 3-5 years since Kate Nilsson's testimony about slug colonization in Anchorage.

My phone rings with urgency as more and more 'green-thumbers' from various locations call to ask the same question: "What do you do about those darned slugs?"

I muster up my best scientific voice and recite the same methods as the Cooperative Extension Service experts recommend. Meanwhile, I feel inner conflict because I'm deliberately omitting parts of the picture. Do I mention how attitudes can escalate the problems? Should I say anything about making cooperative agreements with the collective consciousness of slugs? Will I put off callers by sounding strange or pagan?

I deliberate until I tire of my mental volley. I make time to ask Robert for a consultation.

Ellen: Robert the Slug Deva, would you help me think about something?
Robert: *Yes. I would be pleased to think with you.*
Ellen: Ah, wonderful. I am ready for your fresh perspective. Robert, gardeners ask me what to do about slugs. What do I tell them? So far, I just recommend the conventional tips.

At the same time, I sit on the knowledge that when slugs or any other organism detect a war-and-enemy campaign, they fight for survival. You and the other devas have taught me about attitude and negotiation. Yet most people are not familiar with Findhorn principles of cooperation. How much do I say about this? Do I come out of my cosmic closet, Robert?

Robert: *Yes, stepping on slugs does avoid chemical warfare. But it is abrupt. It would be better for people to offer a rose of peace-making to the slugs. By that, I mean people would do better to accept and love the slug as a God-created part of the Earth, not as an evil enemy.*

If some folks are receptive to more consciousness, they could ask the slugs to cooperate by staying out of the garden and composting materials. We have a phenomenal sense of smell, you know. The scent of a garden and compost is to us like the aroma of bread baking in the oven is to you. It's that compelling.

But we are willing to cooperate, and we can live in the grass and on the edges as a second choice.

Do offer the slugs a sanctuary. Designate a specific area, and promise it as a safe haven. It should have an attraction like moisture, cover, and/or food. Give us some of your food scraps, plus a bit of urine as a smell to attract us.

Ellen: Okay, this helps me. I need only talk about spiritual gardening and Devic consciousness if an individual sounds receptive. I can tiptoe into topics like attitude, or suggest a sanctuary. I need not pour out our whole story. Thanks, Robert.

Now one final question, Robert. Let's say that some people are willing to do all of your recommendations. If they live in Anchorage, can they actually get a decent harvest, especially with vegetables like lettuce?

Robert: (With a sad tone) *No, not if they are serious about market gardening.*

Ellen: That is sad. Hmmm. Well, thanks so much for your guidance, dear Robert.

Conventional Organic Tips for Slug Prevention and Management

- avoid the use of poisons that can accidentally harm cats, dogs, birds, and soil microbes.

- destroy habitat and over-wintering eggs,

- maintain barriers like rings of ash, diatomaceous earth, or copper strips around the garden and compost,

- set out recessed beer traps,

- spray affected plants with coffee

- remove mulches,

- lay down boards, turn them over daily, and step on slugs.

- hand-pick slugs and destroy every day

Slugs –
Does Birth Control Work?

MY PACT with Robert means many extra hours of tedious work. Slug patrol is not one of my favorite activities.

Yet I know of no other management plan to keep slug numbers suppressed. Lettuces and cabbages will not sell if they are full of slugs, slug holes, and slug poop. So I am highly motivated to continue our Birth Control Policies.

To keep my part of our agreement, I check in with Robert regularly. Robert coaches me. I know Robert is always true to his part. This inspires me to be fastidious about following through with mine.

Step one is spring slug clean up. The real Robert (Bob Jones) who is three decades ahead of me in age and wisdom comes out to help me and eventually plants a few vegetables for himself. How I welcome his assistance! We rake. We clear. We pile and burn stalks and leaves. We spray ammonia solution around the edges of house and garden. This took precious time in the rush of spring, and finally we can get on with spreading compost, applying organic fertilizers, and tilling. Now, is it time to sow seeds and put in transplants? No, first we must dust all the beds of each plot with ash. Then we can actually plant!

As summer progresses, I continue to sprinkle ash around the compost piles and garden borders each week. I set trap lines to catch hatching slugs enamored with beer. To lure the teetotaler slugs, I place long boards between beds of rapidly enlarging green crops. The lumber provides a roof and a moist hideaway to slugs during sunlight. Every couple of days, I go up and down the paths and flip the boards. I hunt, stomp, hand-pick, or spray my lured prey.

Has it worked? On this August day in my 11th year, I watch the lid blow off this whole management program. Darn! Looking back, I used to have payoff for all the effort. I rarely saw a slug during those first few seasons. Several years later, I found occasional slugs in the lettuces, and a few among the cabbage leaves. And yes, some slimy representatives slipped by my inspection, only to reveal themselves in a customer's kitchen!

Now I am stunned to discover that Good Earth Gardens is over-run in a slimy slug population explosion. Complaints crescendo from other gardeners all over the Matanuska-Susitna Valley about their slug inundations this season. As I dig fall potatoes, slug adults and egg clusters look like a spilled bag of marbles at the base of **each** plant. As I lift up one 50 foot (15 metre) soaker hose, I pluck 125 adults from under this thin wet line. This is just one afternoon's hunt.

I yell out loud with exclamations like, "These slugs still have more time to lay even **more** eggs before freeze-up! With this breeding potential, next year's population blast will eat me off the premises. Do I have to quit being a grower? Do I have to give up gardening forever? Why even bother to plant a garden next spring?"

Another spring comes, and I am still wondering. Yet here comes Bob up the driveway, generous with his time as always. We rally into our cleanup routine once again. We plant with hope. I watch nervously through June, July, and then August. Miraculously, I spy almost no slugs! Our harsh winds of last winter with little snow cover had apparently freeze-dried most of the slugs and eggs.

I regain my enthusiasm for gardening, and I jump into my twelfth and last year at this beloved location next to Bodenburg Butte. Amazing! I complete the summer with the satisfaction of abundant, spotless crops for market.

Ruthless Alaskan weather can actually be an advantage to a Slug Bargain sometimes!

Chickweed

CHICKWEED INVASION! Chickweed invasion! Chickweed is on the rampage, seeding itself and rooting itself uninvited. Chickweed is advancing, looking like over-flowing green carpets. The carpets fill beds in ever-widening, ever-thickening circles. Chickweed is overwhelming the whole garden... and me.

Each week I battle, struggling to hoe and rototill the chickweed into submission. Despite my best efforts, it spreads everywhere, in every bed.

As the broccoli, carrots, and cabbages attain seedling stage, I find the chickweed becoming much too chummy with young vegetables, growing right next to the stems. I must kneel and weed meticulously with my finger tips, trying not to pull up the tender crops in the process. I much prefer patrolling with a long-handled hoe from walking position, but then I would miss these chums. The chickweed tops pull easily — too easily, breaking off and leaving the roots to eagerly sprout a new set of stems and foliage.

In no time at all, the chickweeds grow as high as the vegetables, or even right over their heads. I tediously part the sea of chickweed to hunt for each young intended vegetable and herb seedling. As chickweed grows older, each plant intertwines its juicy thin branches with all of its neighbors. This results in a continuous snarled mat. Where, under the chickweed carpet, do I place the hoe to get the roots? If I just take my grasping hands and pull it en masse, again the chickweed breaks at the base, ready to re-generate itself quickly... and probably with fiendish glee.

Suddenly it is September 24th. With every clump of chickweed I now pull up, I hear tiny seeds raining down. I am unwittingly sowing next year's crop of chickweed by a hundred fold. Each year is getting worse. The chickweed population expands exponentially, and I get farther behind in weeding.

I am getting exasperated with this species. I do not particularly want to talk with the Deva of Chickweed. I just want to figure out how to catch up next season with its galloping invasion. Sure, a little chickweed tastes deliciously like corn on the cob in a salad. But I do not need a quarter acre of it! Rebellious dreams of herbicide dance in my head.

I wonder if I can ask this pest to tell me how to contain it. That would seem to be against its nature. I get desperate. I finally resolve to make contact and humbly ask this chickweed Deva for management solutions for itself. Will the Deva just laugh at me? After all, chickweed is simply doing what it does to live — prolifically! I am not prepared for the apology and lesson I get.

Ellen: Deva of Chickweed, may I please be in conscious connection with you? I acknowledge your great taste and that you are part of the ecosystem. But as a gardener, I am overwhelmed with your numbers. I will probably have to hire help next summer, just to help contain the chickweed. Do you have any additional suggestions for population management?

Chickweed Deva: *We are very good at holding in soil moisture. As you know, your soil dries out very quickly.*

At the beginning of the season, we do need control. (They conveyed a picture of themselves hanging their heads, ashamed.) We are too much competition for young vegetable plants early in the growing season.

Ellen: You actually feel regret about causing me frustration? That is very compassionate of you, chickweed, when you are simply following your biological dictates. But tell me more about you.

Chickweed Deva: *Later in the summer, we serve you in many ways. When we are among your crops that attain 6-8" (1.8-2.4m), we greatly benefit them.*

Ellen: How?

Chickweed Deva: *Moisture, moisture, moisture! (This Deva is very enthusiastic about its good work.) We excel in helping the soil retain moisture. Without us, you would have to irrigate more often.*

You have learned about dead mulches and living mulches. As chickweed, we are a better living mulch than dead material. Grass clippings can act as a thatched roof, prohibiting rain from penetrating to the root zone. Chickweed, as a living mat, holds moisture in and lets rain penetrate. As soon as you clean out the chickweed, the soil dries up.

We chickweeds also insulate the soil.

Ellen: You do? Is that desirable?

Chickweed Deva: *As the thermometer ranges widely each day now, we* *temper the effects. Think of the difference between a sunny afternoon and the near frost temperature at night. You worry about the chickweed mat covering the soil. You wonder if we shade it from getting enough warmth during the day.*

Actually, the low September sun does not provide much heat. Nor do these mature crops require much soil warmth. It is more important to have protection from the penetrating cold and frost of night.

Among the carrot and beet beds, for example, the green tops still get the sun they need to finish maturing. They do not need a very warm soil. But if the ground freezes, you have crop damage and a more difficult time harvesting. We chickweeds give you a layer of insulation. It is much more beneficial to have us around your crops, than have bare soil exposed to the cold.

In short, we are a living mulch! We nurture your soil! We protect your soil from drying out. We insulate the all-important root zones of your vegetables from the fall frost and freeze-up.

Ellen: Well, thank you, chickweed Deva! This helps me appreciate you more, and curse you less, as I hoe, hoe, hoe! I can try letting you provide living mulch in some beds if I plow you in as green manure before you go to seed. The trick is to observe closely and catch you in time!

Quack Grass –
True Confessions

SINCE MY IMMERSION into Devas and Nature Spirits, I make it sound like I never do battle with nature. I have an admission to make. Reformed though I may be, I'm in full-scale battle with quack (couch) grass. It's a weed! It's a grass! It's Spider Man!

What is quack grass? Some call it *Agropyron repens*. Some call it witch grass. Some call it names I won't repeat. Quack regenerates roots and shoots faster than a hydra re-grows arms. Chop one root and two grow. Cut off a green blade and three more pop up in its place. Rototill a patch of quack and it rebounds in quadruplicate.

Just try suffocating quack grass with mulch — you just challenge it to grow faster. Deprive it of light by smothering it under black plastic? Ha! Its rhizomes (roots) thrive under your cover. They stealthily multiply below, establishing a thick woven mat, thanks to your haven of protection. Quack grass blades emerge from this bunker, thrusting up prolific green shoots just beyond the black covering. Some brave spears of green actually pierce through the plastic itself and into the sunlight.

Spade the soil and remove the snarl of rhizomes, and surprise! New quack grows back from the one-inch (2.5cm) segments you missed. Deprive it of water and witch grass flourishes during drought better than any other neighboring plants.

Quack has about as much respect for boundaries as a school yard bully. Quack gangs establish a base in lawns and edges. Then they invade from these strongholds by Creep and Conquer, silently marching across once tidy borders and into the gardens. Invaders quickly twine their rhizomes in and out of my crops' roots. Don't pull out the quack grass tangle now — you'll pull up your strawberries, tomatoes, and herbs with it. Nor does quack stop with dominating power-plays and territorial take-over. Quack troops actually deploy chemical weapons!

This weed puts out a substance that suppresses growth of other vegetation. What stands a chance when quack grass invades, when starving, smothering, hoeing, and cutting off the water supply does not stop its advance?

Today I am about to surrender two whole plots to quack aggressors. This is another one of those years when quack has gotten ahead of my weed patrol. I cannot plant my vegetables and herbs until I clean out these areas — and spring is quickly passing.

I have no guerrilla strategy. All I can do is slowly creep along on hands and knees, loosening quack sod with a potato fork, and sifting each square foot of soil. I must extract each and every cream-colored rhizome. I take no prisoners to the compost pile. If I do, each little piece will resurrect and gleefully snake into every part of the heap. All my booty goes to the dump in sealed garbage bags. I have filled several trash bags now. I assess my progress. I have advanced a few square feet across one 3 x 40 (1 x 12m) foot bed.

Since I am dedicated to organic methods, I have unwittingly dedicated my life to hand-picking quack. Sometimes I hire crews of kids to dig it. Quack has become endlessly pervasive here. Quack is a parasite, sucking the life-blood out of my slim garden profits. I have another admission to make. I catch myself thinking serious thoughts about the exterminating wonders of *Roundup*. I secretly dream of reclaiming my gardens with a midnight sweep of this notorious herbicide spray.

I am looking for an easier salvation than hand-picking. I comb *Mother Earth News* and *Organic Gardening* magazines for solutions to quack grass armies. I so want to overpower it. I discover a passage regarding some management techniques. One can rototill, cover the area with black plastic, and rototill again frequently, until all the aspiring rhizomes starve. One can also add more artillery: plant buckwheat in the area tilled. Buckwheat has shown some ability to compete with quack grass. Each time one cultivates, the buckwheat babies that are turned under will add organic matter.

Do I try all this? You bet I do! Does it help? Um, well… somewhat.

After years of all this labor and experimentation, I realize I have not conversed with the weed at all. I wonder if my enemy would be so gracious as to tell me how I could do it in?

Quack Grass – Meeting the Adversary

IT SEEMS like I am on first name basis with this weed. I've spent dozens of hours pulling and digging it! I think I know quack well, but I do not have any sense of its spirit. I take myself by the collar, sit myself down, and get brave enough to tune in. It's time that I humbly ask the quack grass itself for advice on containment policies. I ready myself and eventually convince myself to open my heart.

Ellen: Angel of this quack grass, may I please be in conscious connection to you? I am overdue meeting you on this level. I want to work with you. Would you help me?

I have planted buckwheat among your established colony, in front. What is your opinion about the effect of planting buckwheat? Is it doing what the magazine article claims?

Quack Grass Deva: *Buckwheat does aggressively compete, just like we do. The two are competing now, with no winner. It's like they are both elbowing each other with equal strength.*

Ellen: I've been weeding you by hand, rather than using chemicals. How is this for you?

Quack Grass Deva: *Oh, I don't mind the weeding. This is true interaction rather than technological overkill applications.*

I am getting a sense of its personality now. This Being is like a 20-year-old guy who is proud of his weight-training and muscular prowess. He feels good all over, and when he sees an opportunity, he seizes it without a second of hesitation.

Ellen: Why are you so very abundant everywhere — woods, fields, gardens, edges?

Quack Grass Deva: *We have expanded our range so extensively because of human activity. When humans break up the natural vegetative patterns of the whole South-central Alaska bioregion, we are introduced. We are well-suited to take advantage of disturbed soil. That is our job: to fill in all available open spaces. We hold the soil by spreading into exposed places.*

I realize that I had not thought of quack grass as a tool of nature, abhorring a vacuum. Now I can understand how this guy can barge in like a bully, yet see himself as a purposeful servant of the Earth. He will brashly do his job of knitting rhizomes to hold exposed soil. He will firmly harness the energy of the land and sun in an area by spreading his green mat where he can. He is the fixer of energy and the warrior against erosion. I begin to see that my garden and any garden qualifies as a challenge to Mr. Quack. I have created perfect places for him to take advantage and do his duty to Mother Earth.

To confirm my impressions, I ask, "Are you are like foxtail barley — you can be highly successful and so widespread because humans clear land, open the topsoil, and leave it bare?

Quack Grass Deva: *Yes, plus human attitudes. You see us as populous and dominant, but we see us forced to struggle. We respond to the humans who get angry at us and do battle. We respond to the warfare by fighting for our lives.*

Humans of an area get aggravated by us and how quickly we spread and take over. But our driven disposition is not all our fault. The human activity sets the conditions of bare soil. When the humans get angry at us and go into a combative mood with chemical herbicides, we feel driven to survive. Aggression makes us feel that we need to fight back or die.

Ellen: You mean that those negative attitudes are energy? And that energy gets amplified as humans escalate the war with chemical weapons? Thus they fuel a continuous combat? More quack brings more human hate, which brings more war, and therefore brings more quack?

Quack Grass Deva: *Yes, that is correct.*

Ellen: This sounds like the slug's story. We humans aim our wrath at a pest or weed. Without realizing it, we sow our negative attitude into the vicious circle, and fuel a more aggressive spread of "the enemy".

Quack Grass Deva: *That's right! We wish our relationship with people would be more friendly. Our form has many virtues!*

Ellen: Well, let it start with me, Quack Deva. You've gotten me aware and thinking. I hope we can converse again. For now, thanks and over and out!

I sit and ponder awhile. My head spins with this concept of a vicious circle. This is no different than feuds and wars between humans. The Quack Grass Deva is claiming that I am part of the problem. No. That can't be. Can it?

Am I contributing my venom? How much do I act out of anger or revenge? I had better start monitoring my thoughts about quack grass. I'm going to see if I can catch myself and change my thoughts to more positive ones.

Back to the quack-digging I go, but first, I will start weeding my attitudes. Let's see if I can just weed out quack grass in a neutral or appreciative state. I may not see a difference in its growth, but I don't need to feel resentful.

Cauliflower Conundrum

I STEP into an exciting moment. A glance at my garden plan tells me that the very first wave of cauliflower this summer should be ready for harvest. I have not checked on their neighborhood for some time.

Good heavens! What incredible cauliflower heads! They are microscopic. They look more like coat buttons than cauliflower. Why? I am perplexed. I'd better find out. I know these minuscule heads will never get any bigger. Harrumph. They are mature but miniature. I should tear out the whole cauliflower bed and seed in some radishes for the fall.

But first, I need answers. What happened to the dinner-plate dimensions I've come to expect? What should I do about a better yield next year? I start my investigation by attuning to the Deva of Cauliflower.

Ellen: Warm greetings, Cauliflower Deva! My thanks that your form grows here in my garden. I need your consultation regarding these small florets of yours…how can I help you produce giant cauliflower heads for future markets? What special conditions or nutrition do you need from me?

Cauliflower Deva (with a light and airy disposition): When you do your initial soil preparation in early spring for our beds, we'd like extra portions of your organic fertilizers, especially more of your nitrogen, magnesium, and potassium sources.

We need them during certain times in our growing cycle.

Also a mid-season boost of these same organic fertilizers will help. As for how much and when to apply, keep in touch with us for more directions on side dressings and foliar sprays.

Ellen: Aha! So this is caused by deficiencies of these 3 minerals. The cauliflower stems and leaves look spindly, so this makes total sense. Thanks for your understanding and your specific recommendations. I certainly appreciate your helpfulness to me, a beginner. Your directions are very do-able. I really look forward to big-headed results next year.

I start immediately by yanking out those disappointing cauliflower plants. They will not produce any more heads this season. A voice says "Don't do it!" I do it anyway. I am bursting with reformist energy. Not until it is time for fall garden clean up do I learn why I should have waited.

Cauliflower Tonic

Magnesium (Mg) and **Calcium (Ca)** Magnesium and calcium are essential elements for successful and healthy plant growth, maturation, and fruiting. Magnesium must have calcium present in order to function properly. If you choose lime as your source, follow soil test recommendations about which kind of ground limestone you choose. Please see more about fertilizers in Appendix 2.

Harvest and Clean Up – Don't Touch Me

"In the autumn, clean up your garden thoroughly.

Pull up all vegetables, herbs, and flowers.
Remove all debris that will harbor pests and disease over winter.
Speedy cleanup is to eliminate potential habitat for pests.
Fall cleanup prevents unwanted buildup of pest and egg populations.

Make a final compost heap."

THUS SAITH the local Cooperative Extension Service. Tidiness is the recommended practice and all wise gardeners should thoroughly clean up in the fall.

I'm ready! It's September 24, a light frost hit last night, and I've gleaned all I want of broccoli and cabbage. I'm also done with the kohlrabi and cauliflower beds. Now I am impatient to gallop down the beds and yank up all the stalks and stumps. My shredder/grinder is aimed and ready. It will be ideal to process these stalks while they are green, because then they will compost faster and better.

I will feel so virtuous to actually clear the garden this autumn. I have never gotten that far in other years, and always had to deal with tidying in the spring – just when I am in a hurry to plant.

Except that… I have an odd feeling inside. What is nagging me? Shall I ignore it? I'm in motion, geared up to get going! Aw, gee. Maybe I should stop and ask. Maybe Fay is available to check in with me. She can help me verify answers.

Fay is available to tune in. What deva do we address in the garden when my gut tells me something is wrong? We settle on the Deva of Soil.

Fay & Ellen: Deva of Soil, I am ready to pull up the garden plants. I plan to shred them and the stumps, and compost this material while it's green. Is there any problem with this?

Deva of Soil: *Yes!*

Fay & Ellen: There is? What and why?

Deva of Soil: *Those plants have been building and holding energy during the entire growing season.*

Ellen: You mean that I should not rip them up immediately?

Deva of Soil: *That is correct. Avoid shocking them with harvest or removal. Ask before you rip!*

Fay & Ellen: Why?

Deva of Soil: *Because those plants need time to pull their energy back into the soil. The green plants are still alive and have an energy field. The energy needs to return to the soil, from whence it came.*

Fay & Ellen: Into the soil?

Deva of Soil: *Where do you think their energy came from?*

Ellen: I guess I vaguely assumed that greenery is the combined result of the sun, air, rain, soil, and chlorophyll. Plants just grow and die. Wow, I never thought about soil as the main source of energy. You make it sound like the ground is an energy bank. It loans energy during the growing season, and then re-deposits that energy afterwards.

Deva of Soil: *Yes, exactly.*

Ellen: Your guidance is a complete surprise. I thought dead was dead. I thought "soil depletion" meant loss of minerals. I thought "energy conservation" only applied to wise use of fossil fuels. This is a new way of thinking.

Deva of Soil: *Well, of course!*

Ellen: How do I proceed?

Deva of Soil: *If a plant is still green, tell it what you plan to do...before pulling it up. Or speak to the whole row, when you have great quantities. Ask the plants to pull their above-ground energy down into the soil. Then give them time to do this. Finally, rototill in these green plants right there.*

Ellen: Really? I was going to shred them and merrily cart them off to the compost pile. Hmmm. You are telling me something very different. You are saying that I should ask the above-ground vegetables to pull down their energies. Then I do not take residue to the compost pile. I am to turn the plant material under that soil, in that bed. This means I will have less raw material for the compost pile.

How long do I wait before yanking and rototilling?

Deva of Soil: *The timing varies so much. It depends on the vegetable and the phase of the growing season. That is why it's good to tune in and ask each time.*

Right now:

Your broccoli need 5 days of warning, and you can plow on the 6th day. The head lettuce plot needs 3 days, and till them under on the 4th day. They are further gone, and won't take as long to pull down their energies. Your cabbage stumps need only one day after you ask them. The squashes and pea vines have been blackened by frost, so you can pull them up immediately.

Cultivate your weeds into the soil with your rototiller any time, of course. This accomplishes green manuring without carting as much compost to the plot next spring.

Most importantly, remember that everything likes to be told when it's going to be harvested, moved, or uprooted. The later in the fall, especially after frost, the less warning is needed. Each gardener needs to ask about his/her particular situation. Or wait until spring to clean up and gather stumps, as you have been doing.

Ellen: So much for my composting enthusiasm. Are you are saying that some vegetables actually prefer staying rooted until frost kills them?

Deva of Soil: *Yes.*

Ellen: Deva of Soil, I also have quick-growing vegetables like bok, choi and spinach. These early crops have passed peak production by mid-summer. I want to remove the root and stalk residue, clean the beds, and sow a successive crop of something else. What about that? Do you recommend that I ask (or warn) each variety each time before uprooting? Are you saying that I should not expect a consistent rule about the crop or the time of the season?

Deva of Soil: *That is exactly right.*

Fay: Are root crops a different matter?

Deva of Soil: *Yes. Your carrots, beets, potatoes, turnips would appreciate a warning too. They are different because you eat the root part. So you do not want them to do anything with their energy. For example, if you need to trim carrot tops or remove the potato stalks and leaves, then do this right there in the row that you are about to harvest. These green parts will decay and go back into the soil. Again, the energy that is in the roots needs to stay in the roots, because that's the portion you eat.*

Ellen: So we humans are actually existing on the energy of the plants, not just calories and vitamins. That means that quality food is really about the quality of the energy of those crops, right?

Deva of Soil: *That's right. This is what your quantum physicists are telling you.*

Ellen: Okay! Now, what do I ask of root crops?

Deva of Soil: *Ask them to consolidate and stabilize their energy in the root portion you are harvesting. Ask this just before you start digging.*

Fay is given a picture or diagram of the energy patterns in a root crop, before and after the human asks it to stabilize its energies.

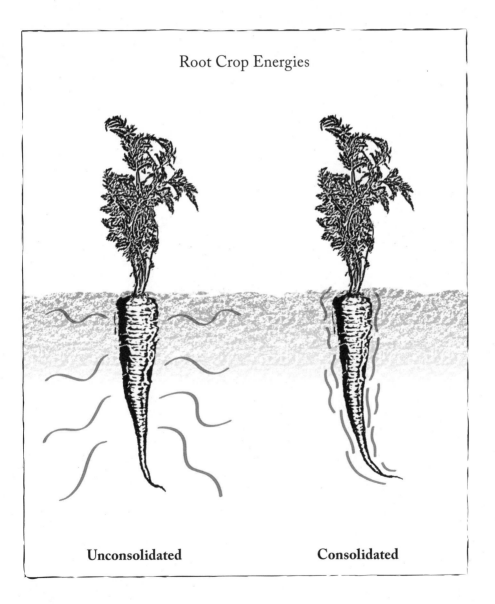

Root Crop Energies

Unconsolidated   **Consolidated**

Fay and I thank the Deva of Soil profusely and close the connection. This message emphasizes how little we humans realize about energy exchange. At the same time, this guidance sounds so off-beam... do I believe it?

Yes. This time I **know** I am not making up answers in my head! I would never have come up with this information. It's contrary to all the gardening advice I've ever encountered.

I am still reeling from this session as I roll my heavy shredding machine back into the garage. Then I set out like Paul Revere to forewarn my last crops that "I'm coming, I'm coming! Ellie the Ripper is coming! I mark up my calendar for the rip-up dates that I have just arranged with the various vegetables.

I guess we all appreciate being notified about things that will be done to us. Among humans it is common courtesy. With plants, it is courtesy plus energy recycling! And if we eat produce that doesn't have much energy, the food is of minimal value to us – no matter how beautiful it looks.

Harvest:

Speak before you Rip!

The wording to accompany the harvest of leaf and flower crops is different from harvest of stalks and vines, I learned. The Nature Intelligences coached me with specific phrases and prayers. You may find these helpful. Please see Appendix 4. In all cases, the vegetables ask that you eat with joy and appreciation.

Beets –
Winter Stockpile

I CLAW OPEN the white plastic bucket lid. I swish aside some dirt and dig in with my fingers. Instantly a stench assaults my senses like three-day old road kill. Is there a dead animal in here? I retract my fingers from the nauseating mush.

I suddenly feel very trapped in the root cellar. I expected a pleasant treasure hunt for some of our delicious beets. I had stored four buckets of them last fall, carefully layering round red roots and soil. Now what's happened to our supply of winter beets?

Get me outta here! This stinking, squishy, rot is NOT going to be our dinner! I smacked on the lid, scrambled up the ladder and slammed the root cellar door.

I had been drooling for the firm, tasty beets we have enjoyed over past winters. I packed those beets exactly the same as other years. They usually stay fresh through March or April. I did see new tops beginning to sprout from beets in that horrible bucket. I know that the temperature in the cellar did not drop below freezing. What went wrong?

I am too sickened and too puzzled to tune in alone. Fay offers her help to consult with the deva.

Fay & Ellen: Deva of Beets, what happened with our stored beets?

Beet Deva (With background music of the Christmas carol, *"The Holly and the Ivy"*): *Some varieties of beets do not store as well as others. Visually you could not see that some of the stems had been frosted when you dug and stored them.*

Try to get the beets stored before frosts.

Fay & Ellen: Ah, so that's what happened. What are the varieties that store well?

Beet Deva: *"Ruby Red" is one. Look through the catalogs and experiment with varieties. Look for ones that claim to be good winter keepers.*

Fay & Ellen: Well, thank you, Deva of Beets. Now we will be more aware and vigilant. Your explanation helps me gather courage to haul those buckets out and compost them... if I can hold my breath that long!

What is the Christmas carol about?

Beet Deva: *Eat up all your winter stockpile of beets by Christmas. We can't last much longer than that if there is frost damage. That should help you prevent the advanced deterioration of later winter.*

Fay & Ellen: Great suggestion! Thank you! We love you. 'Bye for now.

Over the next several years, our beet storage has mixed success. Why? I do not always do my part. I try my best to pull and store beets before serious frost, but I can't always see if the beets have damage from a touch of freezing.

We have learned that the Beet Deva is accurate: if we use up these stashed beets before the end of December, we avoid the stinking buckets. We have a lot more to learn. Still, what a joy to feast on our own red root crop in the midst of cross-country ski season!

Should I Teach About Devas?

MY GORGEOUS, DELICIOUS vegetables are ready! Come and get 'em!

This must be every market gardener's mental shout. What's worse than having rows of delicious greens in prime ripeness and no buyers? These first few years I simply tack up a sign saying "Fresh Organic Vegetables for Sale" by the mailbox. That's my total advertising scheme; I am too small a producer to sell commercially or wholesale. I depend on customers stopping by.

So in my head I keep replaying and beaming out the message: I have beautiful lettuces prime for picking. Beet greens are tender. Spinach is perfect. Please drive into the driveway and buy bags of radishes and rhubarb. These perfect cauliflower heads will pass their peak by next week.

I stand amazed as I watch more people filter in than last week. How do they find Good Earth Gardens? There must be a Customer Deva working hard for me, steering buyers right up to the driveway. Some folks come for vegetables. Some come to talk gardening strategy. Some are attracted to the peace and beauty. Sometimes I can sense the synchronicity when they come. Apparently, this place fills needs. That part feels fine.

What still unnerves me is the questions. Customers and visitors pepper me with gardening questions. What should they use for fertilizer and how much? What should they do about pests in their gardens? What's wrong with their compost pile? I answer with the conventional organic strategies. Then I wonder, should I be teaching people how to garden with Devas? I do not mention Factor X, namely the Devas, Nature Spirits, and tune-ins. Once again, I feel like I'm hiding something.

When I teach organic gardening methods classes at colleges, conferences, and in this garden, should I reveal how to work with Nature Intelligences?

Should I interject anything about spiritual dimensions of horticulture? How can I skip over the fact that I have all these new unseen allies? Is it appropriate to introduce my students to these Devic characters, and their generous cooperation?

I am puzzled. Dilemmas always make me want to consult a higher authority, and this is a perfect tune-in question. Since my pent-up mind-chatter might limit what I can receive, I ask Fay to join me for this session.

Fay and I ready ourselves. With this type of question, whom do we address? We decide to go to the top. We ask God, and more unexpected responses start coming in.

Q: Holy Spirit, should I mention the Findhorn-type relationships with the unseen beings around here when people ask about my gardening methods?

A: *No, that's not necessary.*

Q: I have enjoyed teaching courses about nature and gardening. I would like to do more teaching this year. As I instruct, should I include my experiences with Devas and Nature Spirits?

A: *You are not obligated to instruct others. Your day-to-day attitude makes much more difference than what you try to get others to understand. What is important is your living and being yourself. By that, I mean your whole general approach to living, not just making certain right choices.*

It is the energy and peace you radiate. That is what is important. It's about who and where you are.

Q: This garden has been a personal teacher. It has been a laboratory for learning practical spirituality. The garden has taught me more about the nature of God than preachers, books, and churches ever have. Should I be mentioning the lessons in spirituality that we have been learning here?

A: *Don't make the garden another church. The garden is primarily for you. I will send the ones who need to receive from this garden. I will send them by ones, two's, or three's, as needed. Some that I will send will need to just physically be in the garden. Some will need the energies from the food. Some will need healing from some aspect of the garden. Some will need to know you or other household members personally – the people aspect. Some will need to learn about Devas and Nature Spirits. You will know at the time what each one needs, because I have sent them.*

Ellen: You mean that all I have to do is trust that whomever comes will get what she/he needs? I only need to put forth minimal effort? I just need to feel out what they are ready for? You make my job so easy. If a visitor wants to know about horticultural methods, I need go no farther than explaining organic methods. If a person opens the spiritual topic and keeps asking, I can feel free to converse a bit about the Findhorn dimension. Whew, this is a relief.

Thank you for explaining my role clearly. It's handy to remember that You are orchestrating this show, and the energies of this land will meet those visitors' needs. Thanks for simplifying this — now I can relax and enjoy whomever arrives.

"Bye, Garden"! – Farewell to My Unseen Friends

THE TIME has come. We must put our house and property up for sale. It's the fall of 1997 and Jim is moving out of state to marry. Fay and I are moving on to other adventures.

I must say goodbye to the land I call Good Earth Gardens. I have enjoyed a dozen years of building the soil here. I have loved deriving my sustenance from this ground. I so appreciate how Nature Spirits and Devas have become my personal friends and teachers. I have gratefully experienced gardening as a livelihood. It has been a good life here, and now new life chapters await.

At last, we have a buyer. I am so thankful that this is a couple who appreciate the character of the well-built house and its terrain.. They seem interested in doing some gardening on the 1 and 3/4 acres (1.75 acres = 7,000m²) of land here, at the foot of the 600 (183m) Bodenburg Butte. I will be handing over the care of this fertile soil and landscape to them. I wonder to myself if they will be interested in organic methods? Or a nature spirit sanctuary or slug sanctuary?

We are swept into a whirlwind of inspections, paper signing, phone calls, appraisals, well and septic tank tests, surveying, and a load of other requirements from the bank, FHA, and DEC. Yesterday, the well and septic system inspector showed up. The surveyor came. Oh, oh. Did we tell the Devas we are leaving? Did I remember to warn the Nature Spirits that their sanctuary would be invaded? Fay and I attune this evening.

Ellen & Fay: Nature Spirits and Devas, all of you that we work with at the Butte house and Good Earth Gardens, we greet you with a huge hello! We have been so preoccupied with the mechanics of selling this property. We have been remiss in not telling you what is going on. We apologize. And we are grieving, too, as we will deeply miss you and this place.

We are preparing the house and grounds for sale. That means we must relinquish responsibility to the new owners. We wish we could tell you that they will carry on being sensitive co-creators, but we cannot. It feels odd to relinquish our jurisdiction. Some day, the new couple might be receptive to some spiritual attunement, but we have no say in the matter.

Nature Spirits, we can't remember if we warned you about the parade of inspectors that would be walking through your sanctuary, but meanwhile, we apologize for the trespass of your sacred space.

We have loved working together with all of you. We heartily thank you for all of our mutual learning and adventures in cooperation, communication, and co-creation.. We'll miss your clan and our ways of collaborating as a team.

We wonder how you feel about this change.

Nature Spirits: (With deep, flourishing bows) *Thank you for being a part of this land for these years. Now other places can enjoy you. Go meet our counterparts in other areas!*

As I take loads to the new place, several slugs catch my attention. Ever since our severe winter, our slug population at the Butte had a major die-out and I hadn't seen one individual all summer. (I confess that I did not miss their presence a bit.) Yet here at the new place, I see four slugs crawling inside the lid of my worm box, and another one crossing the lawn in front of where I was sitting. I tell Fay that I am really beginning to wonder about slugs. She and I tune in at the new property.

Fay & Ellen: Hello, Robert the Slug Deva! Long time no see! For me (Ellen) I must admit I was surprised and disappointed to see you, as this means I have to get busy with slug patrol at this new place.

We certainly want to thank you again for all of your love and for teaching us so much at the Butte location. We are selling that property and so we cannot promise you the same working relationship with the new owners. We are seeing your forms here at our rental place, but it will not be the same, as our roots are not as deep here. Our focus will not be oriented to market gardening.

Robert: (With a very warm, open-hearted feeling of love) *We bless you in your move. We feel thankful for the opportunity for cooperating and co-creating with you these past years. Thank you for wanting to work with us, and thank you for giving us the opportunity to experience cooperation. We appreciate that all of us could come together and experiment together.*

Yes, we will be together more, as we are part of the plant/animal community in the Matanuska Valley, but you are right: it will not be quite the same. The energies are different. We are pleased to have been such an integral part of the Butte phase of your living and learning. We love you very much!

Epilogue

I HAVE ENJOYED telling you my stories about cooperation, communication and co-creation with nature at Good Earth Gardens from 1987-1999.

I have shared my adventures with the hope that you, too, will ask Mother Nature. I hope that I have inspired some additional ways in which you will communicate, cooperate, and co-create. The Devas and Nature Spirits are eager to hear from you!

I am the first to admit that the road is not always clear or easy — at least for me. I'm not one of those gifted psychic types. It took me decades of concentrated work to clear out inner gunk in order to begin hearing messages from the Nature Intelligences. Even now, I have many times that I feel uncertain, get no answers, and need a tune-in buddy to help receive the guidance. I urge you to simply expect these swings from feeling adept to feeling clueless, and back again. It's part of being human.

Mastery is elusive and perhaps not something to ever claim. In the great mystery, there is no one defined way to receive guidance, so never stop learning, discovering, and exploring.

When I started this in 1986, I had the good fortune of reading about the experiences of pioneers like Dorothy Maclean at Findhorn, Machaelle Small Wright at Perelandra, Penelope Smith, then in California, and Michael Roads in Australia. Since then, we have witnessed an explosion of spiritual literature.

Today, you have a flood of teachers, books, tapes, websites, workshops, and training opportunities to glean from, and a far more receptive attitude among people in this new millennium. I encourage you to capitalize on others' work. You have more tools and help than ever before.

Your biggest challenge is to use your greatest tool: the affirmation that you are partnering with God and nature. Of course, all this is about remembering that we are all a drop of God, and can go within to re-connect with our divinity.

So keep reminding yourself that you are a powerful and magnificent spirit appearing in a human body. You are colleagues with Devas and Nature Spirits. Claim it, and work for the highest good. I cheer you on as you leap much farther, much faster than I. So get to it! We all benefit from the kinder, gentler world you are creating. I'd love to hear your stories, if you'd like to share them. For further information on classes and workshops you can contact me at:

Good Earth Garden School
www.goodearthgardenschool.com
email: eco_ag@goodearthgardenschool.com

Blessings on all Beings,

Ellen

Appendix 1

Insect Pest Management (An Incomplete List)

First, take time to correctly identify the exact pest. Second, look closely at your emotional approach to avoid falling into combat mode. Determine if the pest's population and damage are truly significant. Third, carefully research the management methods. Consider all the impacts and choose the most appropriate for your situation.

A. Turnip Root Maggot Management

Know the pest. There are two main species: cabbage or turnip root maggot, *Hylemya floralis*; and the seed corn maggot, *Hylemya platura*. They all love the cabbage family also called cole, crucifer, or Brassica family, but can be found in other crops too. For convenience, we'll call them turnip root maggots. They have complete metamorphosis by progressing through a life cycle of egg-larva-pupa-adult fly. It is the fly that lays eggs to start the cycle again. Intercept with controls at the egg, larvae, and adult fly stages.

Floating row covers are spun polyester cloth barriers laid over the crop to prevent the adult flies from laying eggs on plants. The woven material must be absolutely sealed down on the sides and ends of the bed, or the tiny flies find a way inside the barrier. This works if the eggs and larvae are not already in the beds when you plant.

Hand-picking eggs involves a hands-and-knees inspection to find nearly invisible white egg clusters on plant stems, and must be repeated over several weeks.

Inter-cropping means planting a mix of flowers, herbs, vegetables together, rather than dedicating an area to just one kind of crop, called mono-cropping. Intercropping helps to confuse the adult from finding host plants on which to lay eggs. The mixed cropping prevents larvae from conveniently going from plant to host plant and easily consuming the whole bed.

Crop rotation: Each year, change to a different family of crops to grow in that area. Do not repeat planting members of the cole family in the same location a second year. Avoid last year's locations that are probably pre-infested with over-wintering eggs, larvae, and pupae.

Life cycles: Adjust your sowings earlier or later than the larval peak of the turnip root maggot life cycle. Locals in Mat-Su Valley of Alaska have learned that June 7-24 is a peak time for root maggots. With this scenario, plant turnips after July 1 to avoid major damage.

Apply a biological control: Research catalogs for beneficial nematode.

B. Collaring Cutworms

Hand picking or "swish and squish": lightly rake fingers in soil to find the culprit close to the fallen plant.

Collars: Surround each crop stem with collars, or place upright nails or matchsticks against stems to deter cutworms from wrapping around and then chewing stems.

Floating row covers can barricade out roving cutworm larvae. This works if the eggs and larvae are not already in the beds when planted, and if the spun polyester fabric is completely sealed down on all the sides of the bed.

Cultivate: Hand cultivating or last-minute rototilling will foil many cutworms. They get buried and die. Cultivate again in the fall after harvest to bury eggs and over-wintering larvae.

Timing: If you can delay planting until after the cutworms have peaked, matured, and pupated, your crops can grow without threat. This assumes the delayed crops can mature in the time remaining in that season.

Inter-cropping: plant a mix of flowers, herbs, vegetables to minimize cutworm damage to the vulnerable varieties desired.

Leave the weeds: weeds provide food for cutworms. As cutworms eat weeds, they won't find <u>all</u> your intended crop in the mix.

Crop rotation: switch crops every year rather than repeatedly plant the same crop family in the same place. This helps to avoid giving an immediate advantage to over-wintering eggs and larvae. Cutworms don't like all garden vegetables equally.

Sprinkle diatomaceous earth (DE): This is a powder of the fossilized remains of diatoms. Diatoms are single-celled aquatic plants with sharply spiked outer "shells". When soft-bodied insects like cutworms (also slugs and snails) contact this abrasive powder, it scours their skin, causing dehydration and death. When cutworms and slugs eat DE, the scouring diatoms damage digestion and reproduction.
NOTE: When <u>you</u> breathe DE, it damages your lungs. Always wear a dust mask when you are applying DE.

Apply a biological control: spray the appropriate strain of Bt (*Bacillus thuringiensis*) called Dipel®, or introduce a beneficial nematode to prey on cutworms in larval stage.

Appendix 2

Soil Amendments for Sustainable Growers: A Very Brief Overview

It is rare to find a completely whole soil where you cultivate your first garden. To avoid problems of nutrient deficiencies and to maximize crop yield, you will need to apply supplements or amendments to build your soil's fertility. A soil test will guide your choices and amounts. Typically in the first year of cultivation, recommendations will call for a hefty but balanced foundation of soil amendments. To maintain your optimum level of fertility over the following years, recommendations will likely call for amendments in gradually less quantity.

You want the major nutrients of nitrogen, phosphate, potassium, as well as proper calcium/magnesium ratios. You also want micronutrients to be present. The micronutrients are just as vital, but in smaller quantities. Trace element examples include iron, sodium, boron, manganese, molybdenum, sulfur, zinc, selenium, chlorine, copper, and iodine. Finally, you want adequate soil biology and organic matter in your soil. Choose a soil testing company that specializes in sustainable growing to learn how much you need and avoid costly mistakes.

The Goal

Sustainable and organic growers strive to build whole and balanced soil. The goal is to constantly feed and replenish the soil rather than deplete it. The focus is on stewarding the soil, so sustainable growers avoid using chemically synthesized fertilizers. Rather, they deploy fertilizers (more properly termed "soil amendments") that nourish a diverse and beneficial soil foodweb, provide a generous organic matter content, and foster a desirable tilth and structure. They use methods and materials that provide not only the major nutrients, but a balance of trace minerals as well. The aim is to build soil that maximizes plant health and long-term productivity, not just short-term yield.

Chemical Fertilizers: The Effects

Mainline chemical fertilizers do not feed the soil, build organic matter, or promote optimum soil structure. Instead, they generally force-feed the plant, reduce the beneficial soil foodweb and organic matter, collapse soil structure, and cause unwanted acidity and salt accumulation. Synthetic fertilizers are water soluble, and can pollute by leaching into ground water or running off into lakes and rivers.

Conventional fertilizers supply only the macro-nutrients, which are nitrogen, phosphorus, and potassium, called NPK in agricultural shorthand. Crops need micro- nutrients in order to achieve maximum yield, health, flavor, and pest and disease resistance. As crops use up the soil's original trace elements and organic matter, NPK fertilizers do not replace them. Resulting mineral and biological deficiencies leave crops vulnerable to diseases and pest infestation. Then toxic rescue treatments must follow.

Sustainable/Organic Fertilizers: The Effects

In contrast, sustainable fertilizer programs seek to nurture the biological life in soil. Thus they avoid poisons as well as pollution of the surrounding ecosystem. Feeding the soil with complete mineral nutrition and organic matter builds a whole soil. A whole soil is a healthy soil. Healthy soil grows healthy plants that are free of deficiencies, pests, and disease, and have high tolerance to drought, heat, and cold.

Healthy soil is maintained with additions of organic matter (such as manure, compost, and compost tea), beneficial biological additions, and sustainable or organically approved fertilizers. Test lab recommendations determine the amendment strategy and the dosage or application rate per land area. Organic soil amendments can initially be more expensive than chemical fertilizers, but they last longer in the soil. They also contain a wide spectrum of trace elements within them, rather than having to buy and spread many supplementary elements.

NPK Sources Friendly to Soil Biology (and which provide micronutrients too)

Nitrogen (**N**) sources include choices like blood meal, fish meal, fish emulsion, fish hydrolysate, feather meal, alfalfa meal, organic soybean meal, and organic cottonseed meal.

Phosphate (**P**) choices include rock phosphate, colloidal rock phosphate, fishbone meal, and bone meal.

Potassium (**K**) sources include greensand, Sul-Po-Mag, kelp, granite dust, wood ash, and sulfate of potash.

pH Adjusting Sources; Ca/Mg Sources

Note recommendations for ground limestone (lime). It is available as high-calcium lime which has less Mg content, or dolomite lime, which has a higher content of magnesium.

Application

Apply the recommended amendments and cultivate into the soil before planting. Make additional mid-season applications as needed along side the plants (called a side dressing on top of the soil), or by spraying liquid nutrient on crop foliage. This is called foliar feeding.

Appendix 3

The Energy Cleansing Process – A Summary

Strongly visualize each step:

1. Create an energetic picture of a giant filter cloth made of Christ energies. Place it under the vehicle, space, or land in question.
2. State your intent to strain out the negativity with this filter cloth.
3. Picture yourself (and perhaps others) lifting this filter cloth up through the area, catching the negative residue in the cloth as you raise it.
4. When you've lifted the cloth above the item or land, strongly imagine gathering up the corners. Form the cloth into a sealed bag around the negativity you've gathered. Hand this bag over to Higher Power to transform.
5. Give thanks.
6. Pour on blessings to the cleansed area.
7. Ask the Nature Spirits to pour in positive and balanced energies of restoration.

Appendix 4

Harvest – Speak before you Rip!

Leaf and Flower Crops
Ask to be in conscious connection with a particular vegetable. Tell the vegetable what you are about to do and why.

Example "Broccoli in this row, I would like to speak with you. I am ready to harvest you now. I thank you for growing here. May I please have your maturing flower heads to eat?" Now give the plant time to answer, while you quiet your mind. Wait a few minutes until you feel an answer. Then continue, "I thank you for giving your energies to us eaters. We appreciate you and your gift. We will eat you with joy." Then disconnect.

Root Crops
Add this statement before digging carrots, radishes, potatoes, beets, parsnips, and other root vegetables. "Danvers Half Long (or whatever variety) carrots, please consolidate and stabilize your energies in your roots so that I may now harvest this row."

Stalks, Vines, and Stumps
Includes crops such as lettuce, cabbage, peas, cut flowers, cauliflower. Ask to be in contact with that plant Deva. State, "I am ready to remove all your plant remains for cleanup, shredding, and tilling. Please pull down your energies into the soil before I remove the stalks and roots. How many days do you need?"

Close the communication and give the plants time to do this. The longer the plants have been established, the longer you may need to wait (possibly 3 weeks). After a killing frost, wait 1 day. Blackened plants are ready for removal immediately.

As you enjoy eating and receiving the plants' vibrant energy that you have lovingly conserved, give them a thank you!

Acknowledgements

WHAT DOES it take to produce a book like this? Certainly it took my support-ive parents, Jack and Betty, with their enthusiasm for the outdoors and their trust to let me wander the woods. It took having Drs. Mary Jane Dockeray, William B. Stapp and Ronald O. Kapp in my life, nurturing my love and un-derstanding of natural history and ecology. It took experts like Jean Bochenek and Wendy Anderson to teach me about Alaska horticulture.

It took spiritual pioneers willing to investigate new dimensions and then write about and exemplify them. For me, it took Beatrice Lydecker, Eileen and Peter Caddy, R. Ogilvie Crombie, Dorothy Maclean, Machaelle Small Wright, Michael Roads, and Penelope Smith. They gave me glimpses into worlds I did not know existed, but my heart yearned for.

It took you, Fay Wilder, (a pseudonym) to enable my exploration of these worlds. Without your faithful tune-in assistance, your moral and financial support to write, and your initial editing, there would be no book.

It took a gang of unruly angels who prodded me to materialize my experi-ences into a book. That enormous league includes Jean King, Andrea Voogt, Sandra Kluth, Bob and Dorothy Jones, Mia Oxley, Jim Swarts, Ellen Solart, Annie Nolting, Jane Bell, Irene Nilson, Wendy Anderson, my mother, Betty Vande Visse, and all the others who kept encouraging me and critiquing drafts.

Janice Schofield Eaton, it took your imaginative writing skills to change my dull reporting into engaging stories. Alys Culhane, it took your seasoned experience to guide me through the polish and query stages.

Findhorn Press editor Michael Hawkins, it took your weeding and sowing to bring the manuscript into full potential with gentleness and wisdom.

To all you unruly angels in the flesh, my heart-felt thanks for your unwavering belief in me all along, and all your divine help and love. I am forever grateful. May overflowing blessings pour on each of you.

Finally, it took those willing ambassadors, the Devas and Nature Spirits themselves.

I give thanks to all you unseen teachers in the spirit world, (with special fondness to Charlie and Robert). May I continue to receive your on-going guidance, and may I serve as a worthy spokesperson for nature's boundless love and intelligence. Finally, may our human compassion and consciousness awaken rapidly so that we co-create a harmonious new world, hand in hand with you.

Bibliography

Andersen, Arden, D.O., Ph.D., F.S. *Science in Agriculture*. Acres USA, TX, 2000, *The Anatomy of Life and Energy in Agriculture*. Acres USA, TX 2004

Altman, Nathaniel. *The Deva Handbook*. Destiny Books, Rochester, VT, 1995

Boone, J. Allen. *Kinship with All Life*. Harper and Row, NY, 1954, *Adventures in Kinship with All Life*. Tree of Life Publications, CA. 1990

Buhner, Stephen Harrod. *Sacred Plant Medicine, the Wisdom in Native American Herbalism*. Bear & Co., VT, 1996

Caddy, Eileen. *The Spirit of Findhorn*. Findhorn Press, Scotland. 1994

Cowan, Eliot. *Plant Spirit Medicine: The Healing Power of Plants*. Granite Publishing, UT, 1999

The Findhorn Community. *The Findhorn Garden Story*. Findhorn Press, Scotland, 2008

Hawken, Paul. *The Magic of Findhorn*. Harper and Row, NY, 1976

Helliwell, Tanis. *Summer with the Leprechauns*. Blue Dolphin Publishing, CA, 1997

Hodson, Geoffrey. *Kingdom of the Gods*. Theosophical Publishing House, Wheaton, IL, 1987

Ingham, Dr. Elaine. *Compost Tea Manual* 5th ed. Sustainable Studies Institute in cooperation with Soil Foodweb, Inc., OR 2005

Jeavons, John. *How to Grow More Vegetables*. Ten Speed Press, Berkeley, CA, 2005

Kelly, Penny. *The Elves of Lily Hill Farm*. Llewellyn Worldwide, MN, 1997

Loehr, Franklin Rev. *The Power of Prayer on Plants*. Signet Books, New American Library, NY, 1959

Lowenfels, Jeff and Wayne Lewis. *Teaming with Microbes*. Timber Press, Portland OR, 2006

Lydecker, Beatrice. *What the Animals Tell Me*. Signet, New American Library, NY, 1977, *Stories the Animals Tell Me*. Harper and Row, NY, 1979

Maclean, Dorothy. *To Hear the Angels Sing*. Lorian Press, WA,1980. *To Honor the Earth*. Harper Collins, NY, 1991

Nearing, Helen and Scott. *Living the Good Life*. Schocken Books, NY, 1970.

Perkins, John. *Pyschonavigation: Techniques for Travel Beyond Time*. Destiny Books, Rochester, VT, 1990. *The World Is As You Dream It*. Inner Traditions, VT, 1994.

Pogačnik, Marko. *Nature Spirits and Elemental Beings*. Findhorn Press, Scotland, 1996

Roads, Michael J. *Talking with Nature*. HJ Kramer Inc., Tibron, CA, 1987, *Journey into Nature*. HJ Kramer Inc. Tibron, CA, 1990, *Into a Timeless Realm*. HJ Kramer Inc., Tibron, CA. 1996

Schul, Bill. *Life Song: In Harmony with All Creation*. Stillpoint Publishing, NH, 1994

Smith, Penelope. *Animal Talk*. Pegasus Publications, CA, 1989, *Animals: Our Return to Wholeness*. Pegasus Publications, CA, 1993

Tompkins, Peter & Christopher Bird. *The Secret Life of Plants*. Avon Books, NY, 1973, *Secrets of the Soil*. Harper San Francisco, NY, 1989

Tompkins, Peter. *The Secret Life of Nature*. Harper Collins, NY, 1997

Van Lippe-Biesterfield, Irene. *Dialogues with Nature*. Findhorn Press, Scotland, 1996

Williams, Marta. Learning their Language: Intuitive Communication with Animals and Nature. New World Library, CA 2003

Wright, Machaelle Small. *Behaving as if the God in All Things Mattered*. Perelandra Ltd, VA, 1983, *The Perelandra Garden Workbook*. Perelandra Ltd, VA, 1993, *The Perelandra Garden Workbook II*. Perelandra Ltd, VA, 1990

Young-Sowers, Meredith. *Agartha, a Journey to the Stars*. Stillpoint Publishing, NH, 1995.

FINDHORN PRESS

*Books, Card Sets,
CDs & DVDs
that inspire and uplift*

For a complete catalogue,
please contact:

Findhorn Press Ltd
305a The Park, Findhorn
Forres IV36 3TE
Scotland, UK

Telephone
+44-(0)1309-690582
Fax
+44-(0)131-777-2711
eMail
info@findhornpress.com

or consult our catalogue online
(with secure order facility) on
www.findhornpress.com

For information on the Findhorn Foundation:
www.findhorn.org